# SAY IT WITH CHARTS

## THE EXECUTIVE'S GUIDE
## TO VISUAL COMMUNICATION

# SAY IT WITH CHARTS

## THE EXECUTIVE'S GUIDE
## TO VISUAL COMMUNICATION
### Third Edition

## GENE ZELAZNY

**McGraw-Hill**

New York   San Francisco   Washington D.C.   Auckland   Bogotá   Caracas   Lisbon   Madrid
Mexico City   Milan   Montreal   New Delhi   San Juan   Singapore   Sydney   Tokyo   Toronto

**Library of Congress Cataloging-in-Publication Data**

Zelazny, Gene
    Say it with charts: the executive's guide to visual
communication/Gene Zelazny.—3rd ed.
      p.     cm.
    Includes index.
    ISBN 0-7863-0894-X
    1.  Business presentations—Graphic methods.   I.
Title.
HF5718.22.Z45   1996              96–2173
658.4'5—dc20

Printed in the United States of America

    11 12 13 DOC/DOC   0 3 2 1 0

## McGraw-Hill

*A Division of The McGraw·Hill Companies*

**Graphic Consultant**
VERA DEUTSCH

**Editor**
SARA ROCHE

This publication is designed to provide accurate and
authoritative information in regard to the subject matter
covered. It is sold with the understanding that neither
the author nor the publisher is engaged in rendering
legal, accounting, or other professional service. If legal
advice or other expert assistance is required, the services
of a competent professional person should be sought.

*From a Declaration of Principles jointly adopted by a
Committee of the American Bar Association and a Committee
of Publishers.*

## To Ken Haemer

If we define originality as "undiscovered plagiarism," then this book is original. Much of the credit for the ideas presented in this book belongs to the late Kenneth W. Haemer (formerly Manager, Presentation Research, AT&T). Over the years Ken was both mentor and friend. Thank you, Ken. I miss you.

If Ken made me think, then McKinsey & Company, Inc., provided me with a home to apply and advance my ideas. And so, let me also thank the hundreds of professional consultants I work with at McKinsey. It's a privilege and a pleasure.

Last, many, many thanks to all of you who have assisted in making this book a reality.

# CONTENTS

**INTRODUCTION**

# CONTENTS

# SAY IT WITH CHARTS

## THE EXECUTIVE'S GUIDE
## TO VISUAL COMMUNICATION

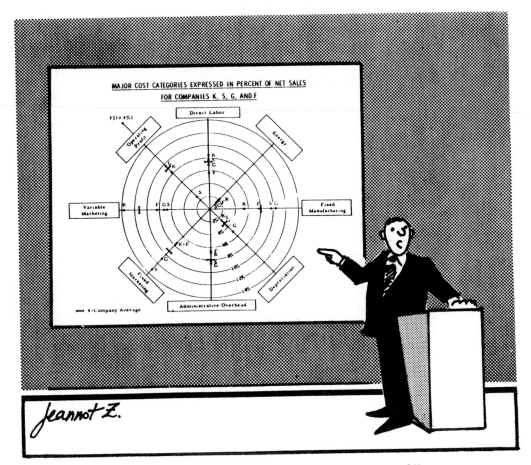

"What do you mean, what does it mean?"

# INTRODUCTION

It's 9:00 a.m. on the third Tuesday of the month, time for the monthly meeting of the Steering Committee. To set the rest of the day's proceedings in perspective, the committee chairman has asked a bright, fast-rising manager—let's call him Frank—to prepare a brief presentation on the state of the industry in which we compete and our company's performance as a stepping-stone for new investment opportunities.

Intent on doing a good job, Frank has done much research, worked on his story line, and prepared a series of visual aids to help him say it with charts. Like most of us, Frank realizes that charts are an important form of language. They're important because, when well conceived and designed, they help us communicate more quickly and more clearly than we would if we left the data in tabular form.

When charts *aren't* well conceived or designed, as we're about to see in Frank's examples, they serve more to confuse than to clarify. Let's sit with the audience and listen to Frank's presentation as we comment, quietly, on the effectiveness of his visuals.

1

Frank begins: Good morning ladies and gentlemen. My purpose is to present a brief overview of our industry and our company's performance. My objective is to gain your support for expanding into developing countries. I've designed a few visual aids to better place my findings in perspective.

First, let me point out that we compete in a healthy industry. As you can clearly see from this exhibit, for the 11 measures of performance shown across the top and the three types of companies within the industry listed down the side, performance is excellent.

*And there you sit in the audience, wondering whether your eyesight is failing, as you try in vain to read the numbers.*

 1

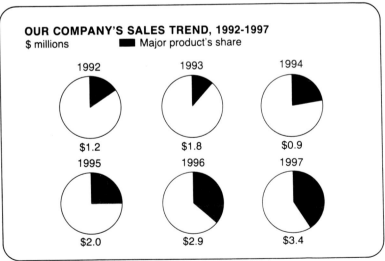

Frank continues: Within the industry, our performance has been outstanding. For instance, our sales have grown considerably since 1992, in spite of the decline in 1994, which, as you know, was the result of the strike.

*"Oops," you whisper," did I just miss something? I could swear I heard Frank say that sales have grown considerably, but what I see is a series of pie charts that show our major product's share increasing. Oh! Wait a minute. I see! He's referring to the figures underneath each pie. . . ."*

▶ 2

**OUR COMPANY'S SALES TREND, 1992-1997**
$ millions     ■ Major product's share

| 1992 | 1993 | 1994 |
| $1.2 | $1.8 | $0.9 |
| 1995 | 1996 | 1997 |
| $2.0 | $2.9 | $3.4 |

Frank goes on: Compared with our four major competitors, we rank first in return on investment with 14 percent. . . .

*"What ranks first? Who ranks first?" you say. "From the visual, I thought the point was that ROI has been fluctuating."*

▶ 3

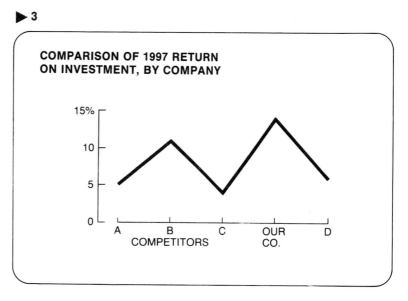

**COMPARISON OF 1997 RETURN ON INVESTMENT, BY COMPANY**

. . . and our market share has increased since 1992 along with that of one competitor, while the other three lost share.

*You sigh in frustration "Has someone spiked my orange juice? Why do I feel that my eyes and ears aren't talking to one another, that I'm receiving mixed signals? Is it perhaps that the visuals I see are not supporting the messages I hear?"*

▶ 4

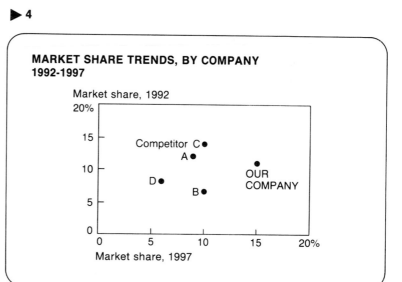

**MARKET SHARE TRENDS, BY COMPANY 1992-1997**

Frank proceeds: Given these sales, ROI, and market-share trends, we recommend expanding the selling effort for our major product into developing countries. We believe these markets hold considerable potential. Since you may not understand this visual, let me explain it. What I've done is shown the total size of the market worldwide in 1995 and projected it to 2000. On the basis of a lot of research, we forecast that the market will increase from $8 billion to over $11 billion. Then I divided the totals by the 11 countries that make up the market and showed the size of each. Then I calculated the average annual compound

▶ 5

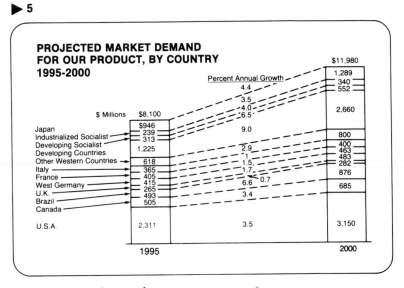

growth rate for each country and listed it in the center. As you can see from these figures, the developing countries are projected to show the fastest growth.

*Now I feel your nudge and hear your aside: "Isn't it remarkable how these visual aids designed to aid speakers require so much speaker aid to be understood. I always thought that a picture was worth 1,000 words, not that it required them."*

Frank: If we are to move ahead, however, we need first to persuade top management that the political and social climate in these developing countries will not interfere with our plans. A recent poll of 16 top management members reveals they are almost evenly split for and against investing in these countries.

*By now, your social unrest is hard to contain, and the pie chart conjures visions of dessert at lunch.*

▶ 6

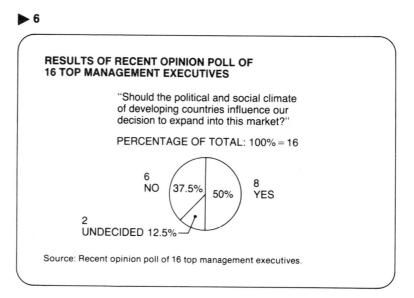

RESULTS OF RECENT OPINION POLL OF 16 TOP MANAGEMENT EXECUTIVES

"Should the political and social climate of developing countries influence our decision to expand into this market?"

PERCENTAGE OF TOTAL: 100% = 16

6 NO — 37.5%
50% — 8 YES
2 UNDECIDED 12.5%

Source: Recent opinion poll of 16 top management executives.

Frank's intention was right: he meant to use charts to support his presentation. His execution was not good: he developed a series of charts that were illegible or unintelligible and that detracted from his presentation. Let's review his charts and see why they don't work.

Visual number ▶ 1 is illegible. Like all illegible visuals, it suffers from the APK—anxious parade of knowledge—syndrome. This is usually the case when the presenter is more concerned with what's been put *into* the chart than in what the audience gets *out* of it.

What Frank didn't realize is that a chart used in a visual presentation must be at least twice as simple and four times as bold as one used in a report. It's the same as the distinction between a billboard that must be read and understood in the time you drive past it and a magazine advertisement that you can study in detail.

At the other extreme is the last chart, number ▶ **6,** which is so simple that it is not needed; the message could have been expressed with words alone. In addition to overly simple charts, there are other situations when you're better off without a chart:

1.  Sometimes the chart denotes a sense of accuracy that may be misleading, as is the case with projections or ranges that may be tenuous.

2.  Sometimes there are sets of data that the audience or reader has become comfortable with, such as the company's profit and loss statement, and changing the form to a chart could be confusing.

3.  Certain individuals may be unaccustomed to, or resistant to, or skeptical about the use of charts.

With charts, a good rule is "fewer is better." Producing charts is time-consuming and expensive. Also, the more charts we use, the less people remember. Use one chart in a report or presentation, and it will receive 100 percent of the audience's attention; use 100, and none will be memorable.

Chart 5, the one describing the world market, is what I call a "charttable"; it can't make up its mind whether to be a chart or a table and decides to be both. The hope is that if the chart doesn't work, the information may. In most cases, neither does. Undoubtedly, this chart helped Frank figure out the important relationships—in this case, the comparison of projected growth rates by country. However, Frank did not translate the data from the form that helped him analyze the problem to a simpler chart that emphasized the results of his analyses.

The remaining three charts, ▶ **2, 3,** and **4,** suffer from what is probably the major problem facing most of us when we translate data into chart form: the wrong form for the message. In Chart 2, pie charts were chosen where a line chart is called for; in Chart 3, a line chart was used where a bar chart would be better; in 4, we see a dot chart instead of column charts.

Here is what these three charts should have looked like to support the spoken message more quickly and clearly.

Sales have increased from $1.2 million in 1992 to $3.4 million in 1997 despite the decline in 1994 caused by the strike.

▶ 2

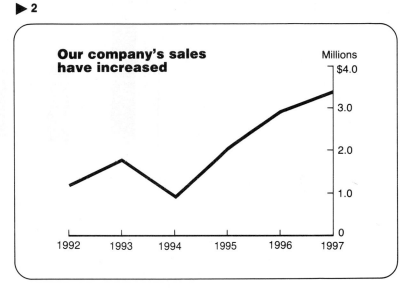

Compared with our four major competitors, we rank first with a 14 percent return on investment in 1997.

▶ 3

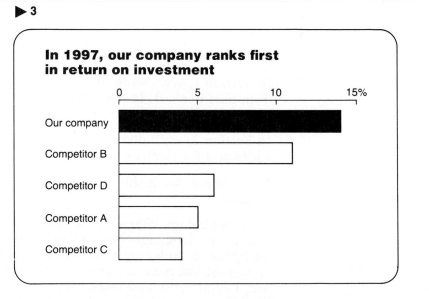

Our market share has increased 4 percentage points from 11 percent in 1992 to 15 percent today. Of our four competitors, B also improved, while C, A, and D lost share.

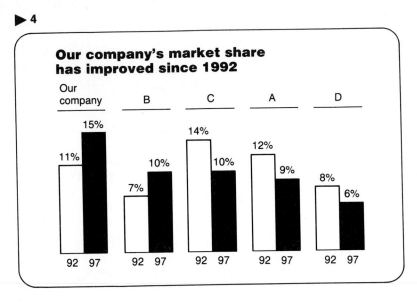

► 4

**Our company's market share has improved since 1992**

Our company — 11% (92) 15% (97)
B — 7% (92) 10% (97)
C — 14% (92) 10% (97)
A — 12% (92) 9% (97)
D — 8% (92) 6% (97)

Now these charts work. In each case, the chart form supports the message expressed in the title, and the title reinforces the point the chart demonstrates. In all cases, the message comes across faster and better than it would if the data were left in table form.

And there you have the purpose of this book. Its goal is to help you say it with charts by choosing and using charts that will work for you and your audience no matter where the charts are used—be it in business presentations or reports, in your management information system, in computer graphics software packages, in annual reports, or in magazines or newspaper articles.

**In Section 1,** we'll work our way through the process that moves us from data to chart. **In Section 2,** we'll examine a portfolio of finished charts that you can refer to for ideas the next time the need arises.

**In Section 3,** we'll demonstrate how to design charts for 35mm slides and for multimedia presentations.

**In Section 4,** we'll show how to convey your message using concept visuals.

As I said before, charts *are* an important form of language. But as is true of any language we want to become proficient in, it takes time and patience to learn the vocabulary, and practice until the skill becomes second nature. Since no one learns by reading, only by doing, I've incorporated work projects so you can practice as you read. So take pencil in hand, and let's move on to the process of choosing charts.

# CHOOSING CHARTS

No matter how many business graphics we see in various kinds of communications—including tables, organization charts, flow diagrams, matrixes, maps—when it comes to quantitative charts, there are only five basic chart forms to choose from. As shown here in simple terms, these are:

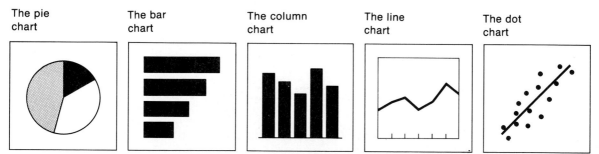

The pie chart | The bar chart | The column chart | The line chart | The dot chart

Now we know where we're going; the question is, how do we get there? With the following diagram, let me summarize the process that moves us from the data we start with to the specific chart we end with.

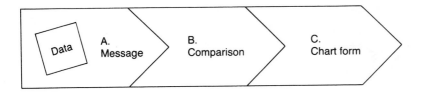

*Step A:*

## DETERMINE YOUR MESSAGE
*(from data to message).*

The key to choosing the appropriate chart form is for *you*, as the designer, to be clear, first and foremost, about the specific point you want to make.

*Step B:*

## IDENTIFY THE COMPARISON
*(from message to comparison).*

The message you've determined will always imply one of five basic kinds of comparison: component, item, time series, frequency distribution, or correlation.

*Step C:*

## SELECT THE CHART FORM
*(from comparison to chart).*

Each comparison will lead, in turn, to one of the five chart forms.

Let's discuss each step in detail.

# A. DETERMINE <u>YOUR</u> MESSAGE

*(from data to message)*

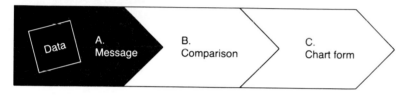

Choosing a chart form without a message in mind is like trying to color coordinate your wardrobe while blindfolded.

Choosing the correct chart form depends completely on *your* being clear about what *your* message is. It is not the data—be they dollars, percentages, liters, yen, etc.—that determine the chart. It is not the measure—be it profits, return on investment, compensation, etc.—that determines the chart. Rather, it is *your* message, what *you* want to show, the specific point *you* want to make.

To stress the importance of this first step, sketch as many charts as you can think of in the empty boxes on the next two pages using the data (percentage of sales by region for each company) shown in the upper right-hand box. Don't worry about accuracy—your goal is to draw as many charts as you can before turning to page 14.

## PROJECT

Sketch as many charts as you can think of using these data: the more the better.

Percentage of January Sales by Region

| | Co. A | Co. B |
|---|---|---|
| North | 13% | 39% |
| South | 35 | 6 |
| East | 27 | 27 |
| West | 25 | 28 |

# WHICH CHART WOULD YOU CHOOSE?

▶1

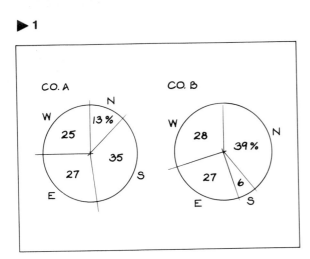

▶2

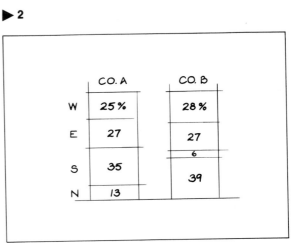

▶3

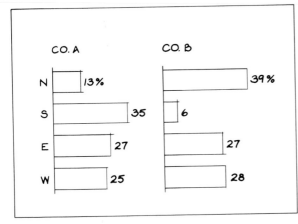

▶4

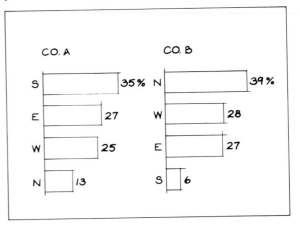

▶5

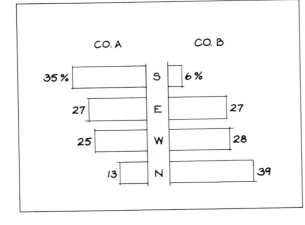

▶6

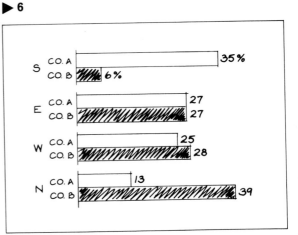

The charts shown on the facing page may be among those you sketched. All the better if you thought of others. But a question remains.

## WHICH CHART WOULD YOU CHOOSE?

**It all depends!** It all depends on the specific point *you* want to make—*your* message. Each chart shown, simply as a function of the way it's organized, is best equipped to emphasize a particular message.

For instance, showing the data as a couple of pie charts or 100 percent columns, you would be emphasizing that:

▶ **1** ▶ **2** The mix of sales is different for Companies A and B.

Or you may have shown the data as two sets of bar charts, sequencing the bars in the order the data were presented in the table. Now the chart is stressing the message that:

▶ **3** The percentage of sales for both Companies A and B varies by region

On the other hand, you could have ranked the percentage of sales for each company in descending (or ascending) order, now stressing the point that:

▶ **4** Company A is highest in the South; Company B is highest in the North. Or, Company A is lowest in the North; Company B is lowest in the South.

By structuring the bars in a mirror image around the regions, we now demonstrate that:

▶ **5** Company A's share of sales is highest in the South where Company B's is the weakest.

By grouping the bars against a common base, we now compare the gaps by region, showing that:

▶ **6** In the South, Company A leads B by a wide margin; in the East and West, the two are competitive; in the North, A lags B.

Now, it's possible—even probable—that in the early stages of deciding what your message should be, you may need to sketch a number of charts that look at the data from various points of view. A more efficient approach is to highlight the aspect of the data that seems most important and settle on the message that brings out that aspect.

For example, looking at this simplified table, there are three possible aspects of the data that could be highlighted and turned into messages.

Your attention might focus on the overall sales trend from January through May; how the dollar value of sales has changed over time. In that case, your message would be that "Sales have risen steadily since January."

**Sales by Product, $000**

|       | Product A | B  | C  | Total |
|-------|-----------|----|----|-------|
| Jan.  | 88        | 26 | 7  | 121   |
| Feb.  | 94        | 30 | 8  | 132   |
| Mar.  | 103       | 36 | 8  | 147   |
| Apr.  | 113       | 39 | 7  | 159   |
| May   | 122       | 40 | 13 | 175   |

On the other hand, you might want to focus on a single point in time. Reading the figures across for May, for example, you might take note of the ranking of sales for Products A, B, and C. In that case, your message could be: "In May, sales of Product A exceeded those of B and C by a wide margin."

**Sales by Product, $000**

|       | Product A | B  | C  | Total |
|-------|-----------|----|----|-------|
| Jan.  | 88        | 26 | 7  | 121   |
| Feb.  | 94        | 30 | 8  | 132   |
| Mar.  | 103       | 36 | 8  | 147   |
| Apr.  | 113       | 39 | 7  | 159   |
| May   | 122       | 40 | 13 | 175   |

Looking at the same May data from yet another perspective, you might focus on the percentage of total sales accounted for by each product. Then your message might be: "In May, Product A accounted for the largest share of total company sales."

**Sales by Product, $000**

|       | Product A | B   | C   | Total |
|-------|-----------|-----|-----|-------|
| Jan.  | 88        | 26  | 7   | 121   |
| Feb.  | 94        | 30  | 8   | 132   |
| Mar.  | 103       | 36  | 8   | 147   |
| Apr.  | 113       | 39  | 7   | 159   |
| May   | 122       | 40  | 13  | 175   |
|       | 70%       | 23% | 7%  | 100%  |

Note that for these last two examples, we used nearly the same aspect of the data to come up with different messages. The decision to emphasize ranking or share is up to you, and that decision will give you your message.

Suppose you have other data from the same company.

This table shows the distribution of sales by size of sale at one point in time, May. Here your message might be: "In May, most sales were in the $1,000 to $2,000 range."

**Number of Sales by Size of Sale, May**

| Size of sale | Number of sales |
|---|---|
| <$1,000 | 15 |
| 1,000-1,999 | 30 |
| 2,000-2,999 | 12 |
| 3,000-3,999 | 8 |
| 4,000+ | 5 |

This last set of data shows the relationship of the salesperson's experience to the sales he or she generates. Noting that salesperson P, with only two years' experience, generates $23,000 in sales, while salesperson Q, with more than twice the experience, generates only one-quarter the volume would indicate the message that: "There is no relationship between sales and experience."

**Relationship of Salesperson's Experience to Sales**

| Salesperson | Years of experience | Amount of sales |
|---|---|---|
| P | 2 | $23,000 |
| Q | 5 | 6,000 |
| R | 7 | 17,000 |
| S | 15 | 9,000 |
| T | 22 | 12,000 |

As we've seen, this first step, determining your message, must be completed before you can select the appropriate chart form. Having spent all that time and energy doing so, you may as well make the most of the effort and *let the message become the title of the chart.* Let me elaborate.

For many of the charts we see, the title is little more than a cryptic heading, such as:

COMPANY SALES TREND

PRODUCTIVITY BY REGION

PERCENTAGE OF ASSETS BY DIVISION

DISTRIBUTION OF EMPLOYEES BY AGE

RELATIONSHIP OF COMPENSATION
TO PROFITABILITY

These titles describe the subject of the chart, but they don't say what's important about it. What about sales performance? What about the distribution of employees? What about the relationship between compensation and profitability? Don't keep it a secret; let your message head the chart. In so doing, you reduce the risk that the reader will misunderstand, and you make sure he or she **focuses on the aspect of the data you want to emphasize.**

Let's look at a couple of examples that demonstrate the difference and establish the advantage of message titles over the topic titles just shown.

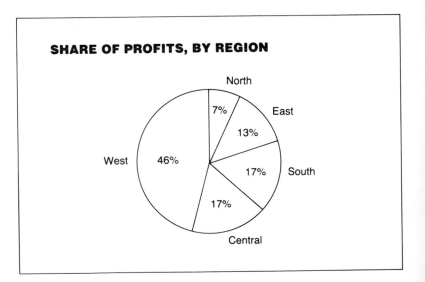

Here, the title states the topic of the chart, leaving you to determine the significance of what the chart shows. Studying the chart, most readers would probably focus on the West, believing the message to be emphasized is that the **"West accounts for almost half of profits."**

However, that may not be the point that the designer wants you to focus on. He or she may wish to stress that the *"North* generates the smallest share of profits." In short, with the topic title, you run the risk of being misunderstood. Substituting the message title, **"North generates the smallest share of profits"** reduces that risk by focusing the reader's attention on the aspect of the data we want to stress.

In this second example, the title merely identifies what the trend line stands for—NUMBER OF CONTRACTS— and serves to distinguish the topic of this line chart from that of other line charts we might see in a report or presentation. However, studying the trend, here are four possible aspects we may want to stress.

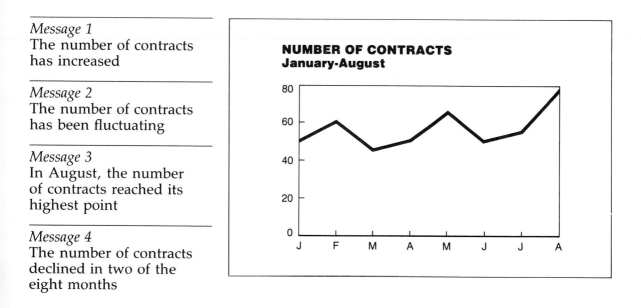

*Message 1*
The number of contracts has increased

*Message 2*
The number of contracts has been fluctuating

*Message 3*
In August, the number of contracts reached its highest point

*Message 4*
The number of contracts declined in two of the eight months

**NUMBER OF CONTRACTS**
**January-August**

To assist readers, let's select **the one message** we wish to emphasize to head the chart.

A message title is similar to a headline in your newspaper or magazine; it is brief and to the point and summarizes what you're about to read. For the cryptic headings we showed before, here's what the message titles might look like:

|  |  |
|---|---|
| Topic title: | COMPANY SALES TREND |
| Message title: | **Company sales have doubled** |
| Topic title: | PRODUCTIVITY BY REGION |
| Message title: | **Region C ranks fourth in productivity** |
| Topic title: | PERCENTAGE OF ASSETS BY DIVISION |
| Message title: | **Division B accounts for 30% of the assets** |
| Topic title: | DISTRIBUTION OF EMPLOYEES BY AGE |
| Message title: | **Most employees are between 35 and 45 years old** |
| Topic title: | RELATIONSHIP OF COMPENSATION TO PROFITABILITY |
| Message title: | **There is no relationship between compensation and profitability** |

Once you've determined *your* message, you'll find the process becomes very specific. So let's move on to the second step, identifying the kind of comparison implied in your message.

## B. IDENTIFY THE COMPARISON

*(from message to comparison)*

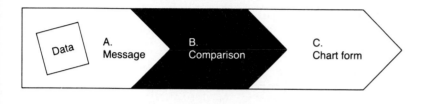

If the first step is the message we start with and the third step is the chart we end with, this step is the link between the two.

What's important to recognize here is that any message—that is, any point from the data you wish to emphasize—will always lead to one of five basic kinds of comparison, which I've chosen to call *component, item, time series, frequency distribution,* and *correlation.*

Let's see examples of messages that imply each one of these comparisons. At the same time, let me define the comparisons and give you clues—trigger words—for recognizing them in messages you derive from the data.

### 1. COMPONENT COMPARISON

In a component comparison, we are interested primarily in showing the *size* of each part *as a percentage* of the total. For example:

¶ In May, Product A *accounted* for the largest *share of total* company sales.
¶ Client *share of market* in 1997 is less than 10 percent of the industry.
¶ Two sources contributed almost *half of total* corporate funds.

Any time your message contains words such as *share, percentage of total, accounted for X percent,* you can be sure you're dealing with a component comparison.

## 2. ITEM COMPARISON

In an item comparison, we want to compare how things *rank:* are they about *the same*, or is one *more* or *less* than the others? For example:

¶ In May, sales of *Product A exceeded* those of *Products B and C.*
¶ Client's return on sales *ranks* fourth.
¶ Turnover rates in the six departments are *about equal.*

Words indicating *larger than, smaller than,* or *equal* are clues to an item comparison.

## 3. TIME SERIES COMPARISON

This comparison is the one we're most familiar with. We're not interested in the size of each part in a total or how they're ranked, but in how they *change over time,* whether the trend over weeks, months, quarters, years is *increasing, decreasing,* or *remaining constant.* For example:

¶ Sales *have risen* steadily since January.
¶ Return on investment *has decreased* sharply over the past five years.
¶ Interest rates *have fluctuated* over the past seven quarters.

Clues to look for in your message are words like *change, grow, rise, decline, increase, decrease, fluctuate.*

## 4. FREQUENCY DISTRIBUTION COMPARISON

This kind of comparison shows *how many items fall into a series of progressive numerical ranges.* For instance, we use a frequency distribution to show how many employees earn less than, say, $30,000, how many earn between $30,000 and $60,000, etc.; or how much of the population is under 10 years old, how many people are between 10 and 20, between 20 and 30, etc. Typical messages might be:

¶ In May, *most sales* were in the *$1,000 to $2,000 range.*
¶ The *majority of shipments* are delivered in *five to six days.*
¶ The *age distribution* of company employees differs sharply from that of our competitor.

Terms to look for that suggest this kind of comparison are *x to y range, concentration,* as well as the words *frequency* and *distribution* themselves.

## 5. CORRELATION COMPARISON

A correlation comparison shows *whether the relationship between two variables follows—*or fails to follow—*the pattern you would normally expect.* For example, you would normally expect profits to increase as sales increase; you would normally expect sales to increase as the size of the discount offered increases.

Whenever your message includes words like *related to, increases with, decreases with, changes with, varies with,* or the converse such as *doesn't increase with,* it's an instant clue that you're showing a correlation comparison. For example:

¶ Sales performance in May shows *no relationship between* sales and the salesperson's experience.
¶ Chief executive officer compensation *does not vary* with size of company.
¶ Size of policy *increases with* policyholder income.

There you have them, the five kinds of comparison implied in any of the messages you'll be deriving from tabular data. Stated simply:

**Component:** Percentage of a total.

**Item:** Ranking of items.

**Time Series:** Changes over time.

**Frequency Distribution:** Items within ranges.

**Correlation:** Relationship between variables.

With this in mind and pencil in hand, study the following 12 typical messages derived from tabular data and identify the kind of comparison implied by each message. Look for the clues—the trigger words—in each, and, if necessary, look back to the definition and the examples we've just discussed. Check your answers with those shown upside down at the bottom of the page.

| **Typical Messages** | **Comparison?** |
|---|---|

1. Sales are forecast to increase over the next 10 years _____

2. The largest number of employees earns between $30,000 and $35,000 _____

3. Higher price of gasoline brands does not indicate better performance _____

4. In September, the turnover rates for the six divisions were about the same _____

5. The sales manager spends only 15% of his time in the field _____

6. Size of merit increases is not related to tenure _____

7. Last year, most turnover was in the 30 to 35 age group _____

8. Region C ranks last in productivity _____

9. Our company's earnings per share is declining _____

10. The largest share of total funds is allocated for manufacturing _____

11. There is a relationship between profitability and compensation _____

12. In August, two plants outproduced the other six by a wide margin _____

## ANSWERS

| | | |
|---|---|---|
| 1. **Time Series** | 5. **Component** | 9. **Time Series** |
| 2. **Frequency Distribution** | 6. **Correlation** | 10. **Component** |
| 3. **Correlation** | 7. **Frequency Distribution** | 11. **Correlation** |
| 4. **Item** | 8. **Item** | 12. **Item** |

Having moved from the data to your message and from your message to a comparison, we're now ready to proceed with the final step—from the comparison to the chart form most appropriate for your message.

# C. SELECT THE CHART FORM
(*from comparison to chart*)

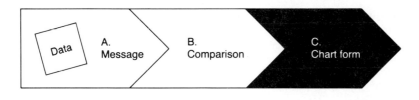

Now you have seen that, no matter what your message is, it will always imply one of the five kinds of comparison. It should come as no surprise that, no matter what the comparison is, it will always lead to one of the five basic chart forms: the pie chart, the bar chart, the column chart, the line chart, and the dot chart.

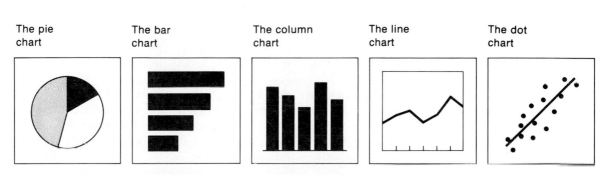

The pie chart    The bar chart    The column chart    The line chart    The dot chart

I've observed that the *pie chart* is the most popular. It shouldn't be; it's the least practical and should account for little more than 5 percent of the charts used in a presentation or report.

On the other hand, the *bar chart* is the least appreciated. It should receive much more attention; it's the most versatile and should account for as much as 25 percent of all charts used.

I consider the *column chart* to be "good old reliable" and the *line chart* to be the workhorse; these two should account for half of all charts used.

While possibly intimidating at first glance, the *dot chart* has its place 10 percent of the time.

That accounts for 90 percent. The remainder is likely to be these chart forms used in combination—say, a line chart with a column chart or a pie chart with a column chart.

Let's recognize that each chart form, simply as a function of the way it's designed, is best equipped to illustrate one of the five comparisons.

This matrix illustrates the primary choices. Down the side are the five basic chart forms. Across the top are the five kinds of comparison we've just discussed. For time series, frequency distributions, and correlations, you have two choices of chart forms. Deciding which to use is a function of the amount of data you're plotting. For a time series or frequency distribution, use the column chart when you have few (say, six or seven) data points; use the line chart when you have many. For a correlation comparison, use the bar chart to show few data, the dot chart when you have many.

Let's work our way through the matrix and see why each chart form is recommended to show each comparison. In the process, we'll discuss how to make the most of the chart forms and present variations for each that provide additional information.

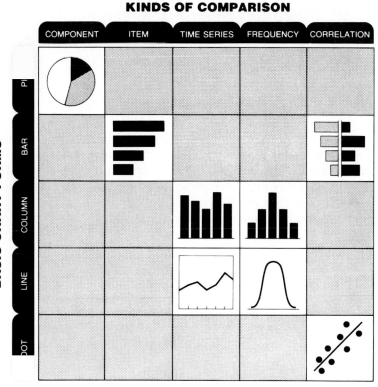

**KINDS OF COMPARISON**

COMPONENT | ITEM | TIME SERIES | FREQUENCY | CORRELATION

BASIC CHART FORMS

PIE | BAR | COLUMN | LINE | DOT

As we proceed, keep in mind that choosing, and especially using, charts is not an exact science. And so you'll note a liberal sprinkling of qualifiers, such as, generally, occasionally, most of the time, some of the time, etc., all of which imply that your judgment must play a role in deciding how best to design the charts. The options presented in the matrix, along with the suggestions for making the most of charts, are guidelines. More often than not, however, you'll find these guidelines will serve you well.

Before turning the page for a specific discussion of each comparison and its recommended chart form, I suggest that you pause for a while and skip to the second section of this book where I present a portfolio of all these charts at work. Browse through this shopping list of charts to gain an appreciation of how effective charts can be when they are well conceived and designed.

# 1.  COMPONENT COMPARISON

A component comparison can best be demonstrated using a pie chart. Because a circle gives such a clear impression of being a total, a pie chart is ideally suited for the one—and only—purpose it serves: showing the size of each part as a percentage of some whole, such as companies that make up an industry.

**THE PIE CHART**

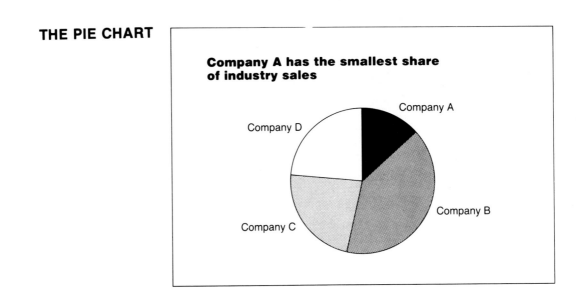

To make the most of pie charts, you should generally use not more than six components. If you have more than six, select the five components most important to your message and group the remainder into an "others" category.

Because the eye is accustomed to measuring in a clockwise motion, position the most important segment against the 12 o'clock line and, to add emphasis, use the most contrasting color (e.g., yellow against a black background), or the most intense shading pattern if producing the chart in black and white. If no one segment is more important than the others, consider arranging the components from the largest to the smallest or vice versa and use either the same color or no shading for all segments.

In general, pie charts are the least practical of the five chart forms. They are also the most misused and, worse, the most abused.

For example, on the next page are several pseudo pie charts I've discovered over the years in various presentations, newspapers, magazines, and annual reports. Now I'll grant you each is imaginative and resourceful, even attractive, although example D is a bit macabre. They are also examples of form becoming more important than content and, as a result, they fail to present accurate visual relationships.

Let me stress that the primary purpose of any chart is to demonstrate relationships more quickly and more clearly than is possible using a tabular form. Whenever the form becomes more important than the content—that is, whenever the design of the chart interferes with a clear grasp of the relationship—it does a disservice to the audience or readers who may be basing decisions on the strength of what they see.

Let's have fun and do an exercise that tests the usefulness of these examples as visual *aids*. To get the most from the following work project, promise that *you will not think;* record your first visual impression. For each example, starting at the top and moving down or around, quickly fill in the percentage of the total corresponding to each component. Then add the totals. Most important, you CAN'T GO BACK, you CAN'T ERASE, and fortunately you CAN'T CHANGE YOUR MIND, since you cannot think.

GO!

For each of these six charts, fill in the percentage you feel each
segment represents and add them up.

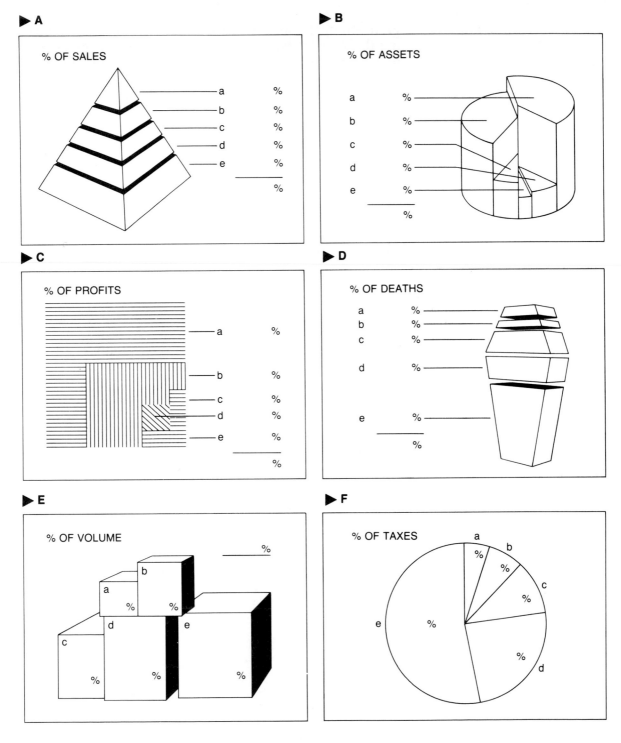

► A

% OF SALES

a     %
b     %
c     %
d     %
e     %
_____
%

► B

% OF ASSETS

a     %
b     %
c     %
d     %
e     %
_____
%

► C

% OF PROFITS

a     %
b     %
c     %
d     %
e     %
_____
%

► D

% OF DEATHS

a     %
b     %
c     %
d     %
e     %
_____
%

► E

% OF VOLUME

%
a   %   %
b
c   d   e
%   %   %

► F

% OF TAXES    a
    b
  %
   %
    c
   %
e    %
   %
  d

Now compare all your guesses with the actual data that accompanied each example:

| | A<br>Percent of sales | B<br>Percent of assets | C<br>Percent of profits | D<br>Percent of deaths | E<br>Percent of volume | F<br>Percent of taxes |
|---|---|---|---|---|---|---|
| a. | 5% | 37% | 58% | 7% | 7% | 5% |
| b. | 7 | 31 | 32 | 6 | 15 | 7 |
| c. | 11 | 10 | 3 | 17 | 18 | 11 |
| d. | 24 | 14 | 4 | 16 | 25 | 24 |
| e. | 53 | 8 | 3 | 54 | 35 | 53 |
| | 100% | 100% | 100% | 100% | 100% | 100% |

If your results were radically different from these numbers—at least for Charts A through E—then it's clear that the charts are not doing the job they were intended to do, which is to give you an *accurate* impression of the relationships. I've tested these with many colleagues. Chances are your results were similar to theirs. In few cases did the data add to exactly 100 percent. Instead, the components added to less than 100 percent as often as they did to well over 100 percent. In the most extreme cases, the data added up to only 45 percent at the lower end and to 280 percent at the high end. Even when people arrived at the same total, their proportions were not necessarily similar.

On the other hand, almost everyone was accurate in estimating the percentages in Example F, *Percent of Taxes,* presented as a conventional pie chart. Here, people could more readily *see* that segment *a* is somewhere around 5 percent and that *d* is about 25 percent, while *e* is a bit more than 50 percent. In truth, Example F is based on the same data as Example A. I just changed the titles to see what would happen. Compare the percentage values you filled in for A with those you wrote for F and note how the difference in chart form threw you off.

There's a clear lesson to be learned from this exercise: If your objective is to communicate accurate relationships, overcome the urge to be creative and instead rely on conventional pie charts. Use your creativity to make the charts attractive with handsome layouts, readable type, and constructive use of color or shadings.

A pie chart serves the purpose of showing the components of a single total better than a 100 percent bar or 100 percent column chart. However, as soon as you need to compare the components of more than one total, don't think, don't hesitate. Switch to either 100 percent bars or 100 percent columns. This example shows why.

**Poor**                                                    **Preferred**

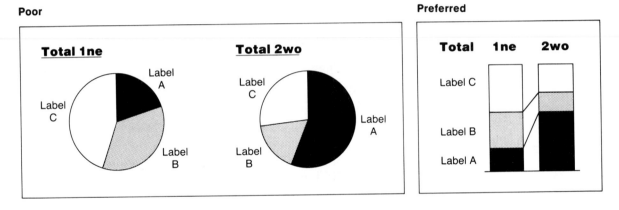

Notice how the labels must be repeated for each of the two pie charts shown. Of course, we could use a legend. However, this forces the reader to look back and forth between the legend and the components to be clear about which belongs to which. Also, although shadings—or colors—help the viewer to distinguish the three components, the eyes must travel back and forth, from pie to pie, to grasp the relationships.

By using two 100 percent columns instead, we reduce the problems. Now the labeling is less redundant, and the relationships between corresponding segments, here reinforced with connecting lines, are more quickly apparent.

## 2. ITEM COMPARISON

An item comparison can best be demonstrated by a bar chart.

The vertical dimension is not a scale; all it is used for is labeling the measured items—such as countries, industries, companies, salespeople's names. This being the case, you can arrange the bars in any sequence that suits the ranking you want to stress. For example, in a chart that compares the return on sales for a client company with that of its five competitors at one point in time, the bars can be sequenced by company name in alphabetical order, or by date of entry into the industry, or by size of sales, or by the magnitude of the return from either low to high or, as in this example, from high to low (from best to worst).

**THE BAR CHART**

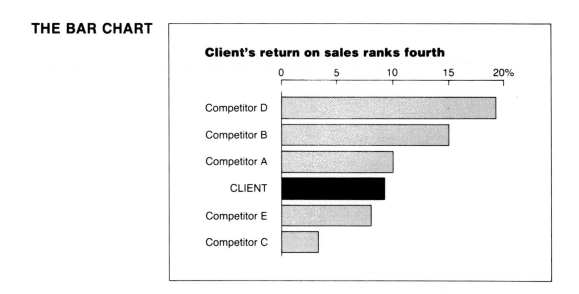

In preparing bar charts, make certain that the space separating the bars is smaller than the width of the bars. Use the most contrasting color or shading to emphasize the important item, thereby reinforcing the message title.

To identify the values, use either a scale at the top (sometimes at the bottom) or numbers at the ends of the bars, not both. Use the scale if all you want is a fast study of the relationships; use the numbers if they are important to your message. At times, it's a good idea to use the scale and *the one number* that needs emphasis. Using both scale and numbers, however, is redundant and adds clutter to the bar chart, as it does, for that matter, to the column chart and the line chart.

When showing numbers, round out the figures and omit decimals whenever they have little effect on your message; a figure such as 12 percent is more easily retained than 12.3 percent or 12.347 percent.

To demonstrate the versatility of the bar chart, here are six variations of the chart form, each providing additional information. Examples of the application of these variations are illustrated in Section 2 of this book. You may want to glance at them now. Certainly you will want to incorporate them into your vocabulary of charts at work.

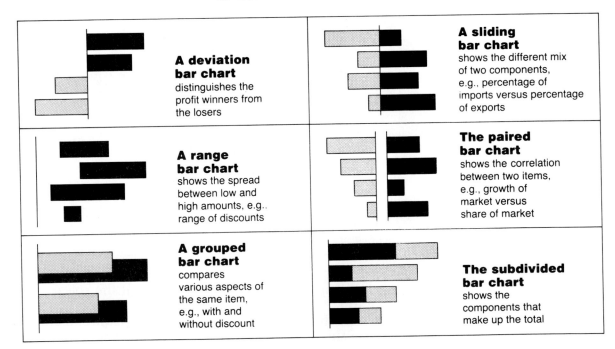

**A deviation bar chart** distinguishes the profit winners from the losers

**A sliding bar chart** shows the different mix of two components, e.g., percentage of imports versus percentage of exports

**A range bar chart** shows the spread between low and high amounts, e.g.. range of discounts

**The paired bar chart** shows the correlation between two items, e.g., growth of market versus share of market

**A grouped bar chart** compares various aspects of the same item, e.g., with and without discount

**The subdivided bar chart** shows the components that make up the total

At times, you may want to use the column chart instead of the bar chart—vertical bars instead of horizontal bars—to show an item comparison. There's really nothing violently wrong with doing so. However, 9 times out of 10, you're better off with the bar chart for two reasons. First, by reserving bar charts for showing an item comparison, we reduce the possibility of confusion with a time series comparison, for which column charts are more appropriate. To reinforce this distinction, therefore, let's avoid using the bar chart for showing changes over time; in Western culture, we're accustomed to thinking of time moving from left to right, not top to bottom.

The second reason is a practical one. Generally, items have lengthy labels—territories such as Northeast, Southwest; industries such as agriculture, manufacturing; salespeople's names—all requiring space. Notice from the two examples shown that you have all the space you need to the left of the bars to label the various items, whereas, with the column chart, you may have to go through contortions since columns are usually narrow. Here you have to squeeze the label to the point of illegibility, or hyphenate the word, or write it in an awkward manner.

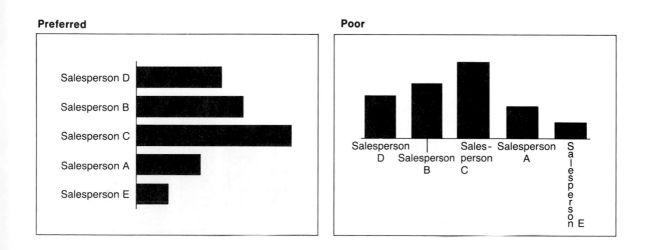

## 3. TIME SERIES COMPARISON

Whereas a component comparison and an item comparison show relationships at one point in time, the time series comparison shows changes over time.

A time series comparison can best be demonstrated with either a column chart or a line chart. Deciding on which to use is simple. If you have only a few points in time to plot (say, up to seven or eight) use the column chart; if, on the other hand, you have to show a trend over 20 years by quarters, you're much better off with the line chart.

In choosing between a column and a line chart, you can also be guided by the nature of the data. A column chart emphasizes levels or magnitudes and is more suitable for data on activities that occur within a set period of time, suggesting a fresh start for each period. Production data fit into this category. A line chart emphasizes movement and angles of change and is therefore the best form for showing data that have a "carry-over" from one time to the next. A good example here is inventory data.

Beyond these distinctions, each chart form has its own characteristics and variations, so let's study them separately.

**THE COLUMN CHART**

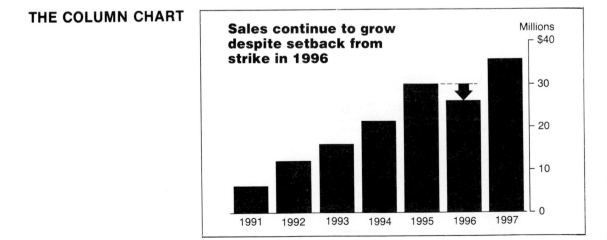

Sales continue to grow despite setback from strike in 1996

The suggestions for making the most of bar charts also apply to column charts: make the space between the columns smaller than the width of the columns; and use color or shading to emphasize one point in time more than others or to distinguish, say, historical from projected data.

As with the bar chart, there are several variations of the column chart that make it a resourceful and valuable tool; these variations are shown at work in Section 2.

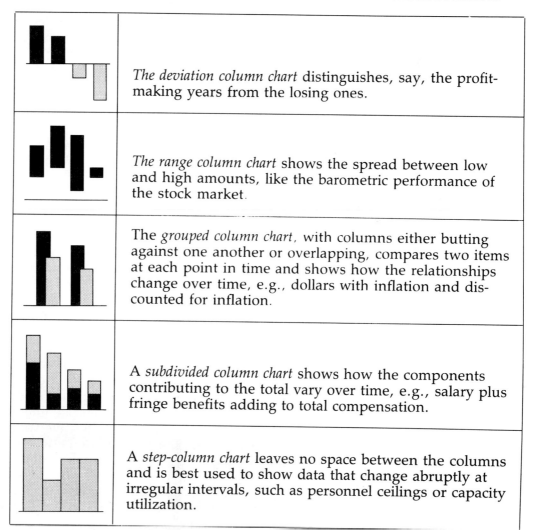

*The deviation column chart* distinguishes, say, the profit-making years from the losing ones.

*The range column chart* shows the spread between low and high amounts, like the barometric performance of the stock market.

The *grouped column chart*, with columns either butting against one another or overlapping, compares two items at each point in time and shows how the relationships change over time, e.g., dollars with inflation and discounted for inflation.

A *subdivided column chart* shows how the components contributing to the total vary over time, e.g., salary plus fringe benefits adding to total compensation.

A *step-column chart* leaves no space between the columns and is best used to show data that change abruptly at irregular intervals, such as personnel ceilings or capacity utilization.

## THE LINE CHART

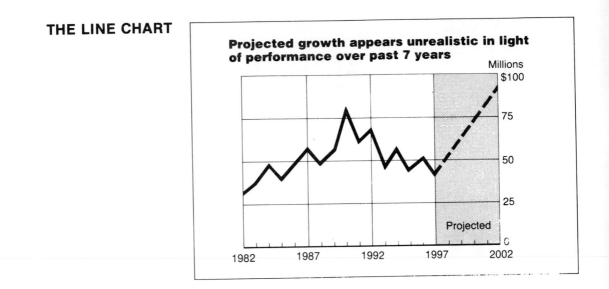

**Projected growth appears unrealistic in light of performance over past 7 years**

Millions
$100
75
50
25
0

Projected

1982    1987    1992    1997    2002

Without doubt, the line chart is the most often used of the five charts, and well it should be since it is the easiest to draw, the most compact, and the clearest for discerning whether the trend is increasing, decreasing, fluctuating, or remaining constant.

When preparing a line chart, make sure the trend line is bolder than the baseline and that the baseline, in turn, is a little bit heavier than the vertical and horizontal scale lines that shape the reference grid.

Think of grid rulings as you would the umpire at a sporting event; they're there for reference purposes, not to dominate the main attraction—in this case, the trend line(s). In other words, you may use vertical grid lines to distinguish the historic from the projected, or to emphasize quarterly periods, or to separate five-year increments. Similarly, a few horizontal scale lines will make it easier for the reader to discern relative values. In short, use your judgment to choose between too many and none at all.

The line chart has only two variations, far fewer than the bar chart or the column chart, but important enough to deserve more discussion.

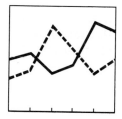

*The grouped line chart* compares the performance of two or more items. To distinguish, say, your company's trend from those of your competitors', use the most contrasting color or the boldest solid line for your company and less intense colors or thinner or patterned lines (long dashes, short dashes) for the others.

The challenge is deciding how many trend lines we can show simultaneously before the chart looks more like spaghetti than trends. Let's be realistic, a line chart with eight trend lines isn't necessarily twice as useful as one with four lines; twice as confusing, maybe, but not twice as useful.

A technique for untangling the mess is to pair your trend with that of each competitor on a set of smaller charts, as you see. Granted, this creates more charts, but simpler comparisons per chart.

**The Spaghetti Chart**

**Untangling the Mess**

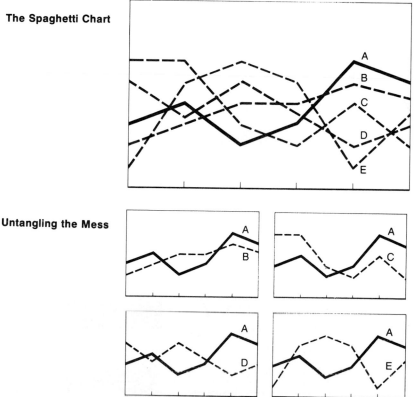

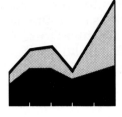

By coloring or shading the surface between the trend line and the baseline, we create the *surface chart*. By subdividing the surface into the components that make up the totals at each point in time, we create the *subdivided surface chart*. Here too, as with the subdivided bar and column charts, limit the number of layers to five or fewer. If there are more than five segments, plot only the four important ones and group the remaining into an "others" category.

For all subdivided charts, place the most important segment against the baseline, since this is the only segment that is measured against a straight line. All other segments are at the mercy of the ups and downs of that segment.

As with the spaghetti chart we just discussed, the technique for making sense of the sea of layers is to separate the components and show each on its own base, reducing the subdivided chart to simpler surface charts.

**From Subdivided Line Chart**

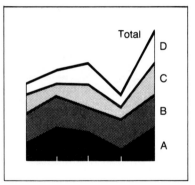

**To Simpler Surface Charts**

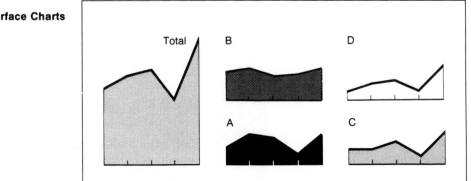

## 4. FREQUENCY DISTRIBUTION COMPARISON

A frequency distribution comparison shows how many items (frequency) fall into a series of progressive numerical ranges (distribution).

There are two major applications for this kind of comparison. The first is generalizing likely events on the basis of a sample of observations. Here, the frequency distribution is used to predict risk, probability, or chance. One use might be to show that there is a 25 percent chance that shipments will be delivered in five days or less; another might be to describe (un)certainty, such as the odds of rolling a losing seven, as a percentage of all possible outcomes, when shooting craps. (Save your money, the odds are one in six.)

**% of all possible outcomes**

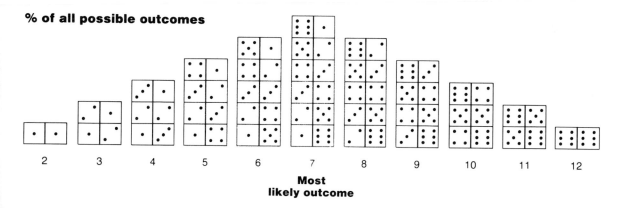

**Most
likely outcome**

The "bell-shaped" curves and frequency polygons that are associated with this application are governed by mathematical rules. Do yourself a favor and rely on the assistance of a statistician to design them. Since these "curves" are used primarily for analytical purposes, they are not our concern in this book.

The second application, often seen in business presentations and reports, is summarizing vast amounts of data to demonstrate some meaningful relationship (e.g., 25 percent of the shipments are delivered in five to six days). This application is particularly useful for demographic information such as the number of employees by salary ranges, or the distribution of U.S. families by income levels, or the voting pattern by age group. As you would expect, this use of frequency distribution gains in popularity each time the national census is taken and every four years along with presidential elections.

In this role, the frequency distribution can best be shown by either a *step-column chart* (*histogram*) or a *line chart* (*histograph*). Column charts are better when only a few ranges are used—say, five or seven—and line charts are better when there are many.

## THE COLUMN CHART (HISTOGRAM)

**75% of our employees earn more than $30,000**

Number of employees

## THE LINE CHART (HISTOGRAPH)

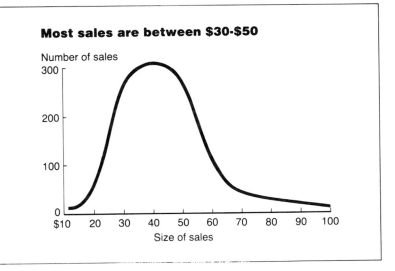

**Most sales are between $30-$50**

Number of sales

These charts have two scales: the vertical one (frequency) is for the number (sometimes percentage) of items or occurrences; the horizontal one (distribution) is for the ranges. The distribution scale requires special attention.

*Size of the Ranges.*   The size of the ranges—and therefore the number of groups—is important in bringing out the pattern of the distribution. Too few groups hide the pattern; too many groups break it up. As a general rule, use no fewer than 5 groups and no more than 20. Within these extremes, however, you're looking for the number of groups that will demonstrate your intended message. For instance, if we wanted to bring out the pattern of a distribution of average annual salaries paid to public school teachers in the 50 states:

Grouping the ranges by $500 increments reveals no discernible pattern.

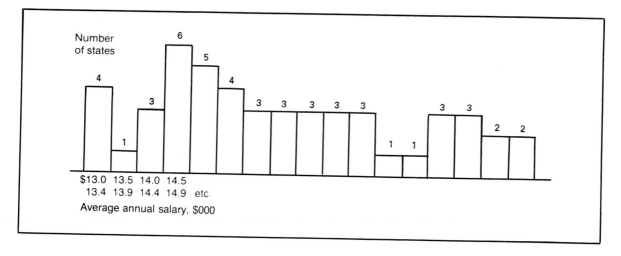

Grouping the ranges by $1,000 increments begins to suggest a pattern.

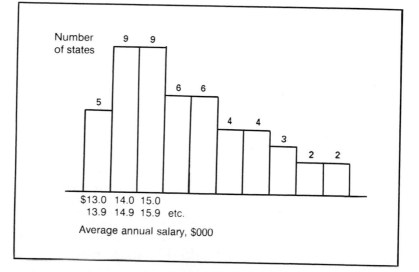

But it isn't until we group the ranges by $2,000 increments that we clearly see the bell-shaped curve usually associated with a frequency distribution. In this example, the curve is skewed to the left—that is, to the lower side of the distribution—indicating a possible message that almost half of the states (23 states out of 50) paid their teachers less than $16,000 in the year.

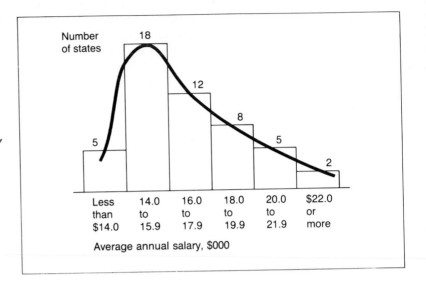

*Size of the Groups.* It is best to use groups of equal size. If one grouping represented a $5 range and the next, $20, the shape of the distribution would be distorted. Among the exceptions are cases where the data are not recorded in equal steps (e.g., educational levels) or where unequal steps make better sense, such as personal income tax brackets. Because the range of incomes is so great, and because there are so many people near the lower end and so few near the upper end, equal intervals won't work; $1,000 intervals would result in a chart several yards wide, $40,000 intervals would put virtually everyone in the first interval. The chart would be more informative if smaller intervals were shown at the lower end and larger ranges at the upper end.

*Clear Labeling.* The size of the groups should be explained clearly. "Overlapping" labels, such as 0–10, 10–20, 20–30, do not tell which groups include the repeated figure. For continuous data, such as dollar sales, the preferred method is less than $10.00, $10.00–19.99, $20.00–29.99, etc. For discrete data, such as number of cars manufactured, the preferred method is less than 10, 10–19, 20–29, etc.

Both the histogram and the histograph can be grouped to show, for instance, the distribution for one year against another, or to compare your employees' age distribution with that of a competitor or perhaps an industry average. Also, when absolute numbers are used, they can be subdivided to show how the components add to their total.[1]

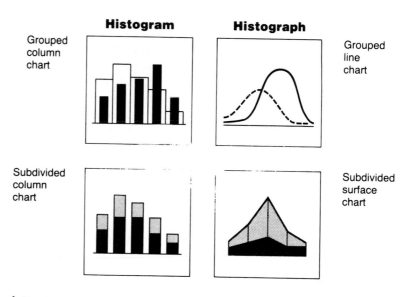

**Histogram**  **Histograph**

Grouped column chart

Grouped line chart

Subdivided column chart

Subdivided surface chart

[1] *Caution:* It is misleading to subdivide a frequency distribution when the frequency is expressed in percentage terms. For example, if 60 percent of women earn between, say, $5 and $10 an hour, and 50 percent of men earn the same, it cannot be said that combined, 110 percent of the people earn between $5 and $10 an hour.

# 5. CORRELATION COMPARISON

A correlation comparison shows whether the relationship between two variables follows—or fails to follow—the pattern you would normally expect. For example, you would normally expect that a salesperson with more experience would generate more sales than one with less experience; you would normally expect that employees with more education would receive higher starting salaries. Such comparisons are best shown by a dot chart, sometimes called a scatter diagram, or by a paired bar chart. Let's look at each in turn.

**THE DOT CHART**

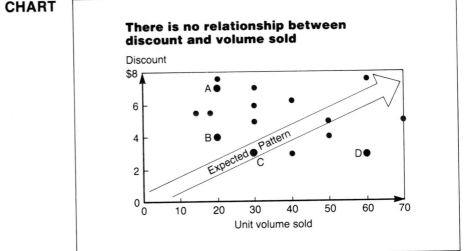

Here we show 16 transactions in terms of the size of the discount offered and the number of units sold. Normally, you would expect that the larger the discount, the greater the incentive to purchase more units. As the dot chart reveals in this case, there is no such correlation.

For instance, study the dots labeled *A* and *B*, representing the transactions of two salespeople. Both sold 20 units (horizontal scale). However, *A* offered a $7 discount, while *B* gave only $4 (vertical scale). On the other hand, salespeople *C* and *D* offered the same $3 discount, and yet *C* sold 30 units while *D* sold twice as many. Obviously, the size of the discount offered has little or no effect on the volume bought.

Had there been a correlation, then the dots would have clustered around a diagonal line moving from the lower left of the chart to the upper right, represented here by a faint background arrow. It's often a good idea to include this arrow to reinforce the expected pattern. Of course, at times, the arrow might point down to show, for example, that volume increases as price decreases. Also, let's not confuse this arrow with the mathematically computed "line of best fit," which is a curve fitted through the dots that emphasizes the pattern of the plotted values.

These dot charts are being used increasingly in presentations, reports, and some business magazines. If you plan to use them, be patient with your audience or reader and explain how to read the chart before revealing the message.

Aside from appearing confusing, the problem with these charts is identifying the dots. Including each salesperson's name next to his or her dot not only adds to the confusion but can create a severe case of myopia. An option is to use a legend with each dot identified by a letter or number corresponding to the full name shown somewhere else on the chart. A better option is to use the paired bar chart.

## THE BAR CHART

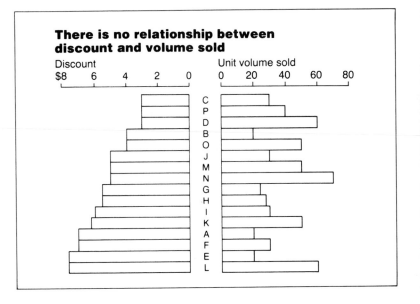

**There is no relationship between discount and volume sold**

You'll notice that now there is space to label each set of plotted values between the sets of bars. In a paired bar chart, we usually rank the independent variable on the left, in either a low-to-high or high-to-low sequence. When the relationship between the expected pattern and the actual one is consistent, the dependent variable bars on the right will form a mirror image of those on the left. In other words, low discounts will mirror low volume and high discounts will be paired with high volume. When the relationship is not as expected, the two sets of bars will deviate from one another, as they do in this example.

This paired bar chart option will work only when there are relatively few sets of data to plot. Beyond 15 or so, you're better off with the more compact scatter diagram and forgetting about trying to label each dot.

While there are no variations for the paired bar chart, there are several worth mentioning for the dot chart.

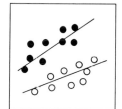 The *grouped dot chart* shows the correlation of two items or of one item at different times. Although solid and open dots are used here, other suitable symbols, such as squares, triangles, or stars, can also be used.

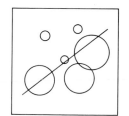 A third variable is introduced in the *bubble chart* with dots of different sizes. For instance, where the two scales might represent sales and profits, the size of the dot might indicate the relative size of assets for each company in an industry.

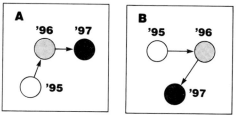 The *time dot chart* shows the change over time of the correlation. Avoid the tendency to show all such movements on one grid; instead, place each on its own chart.

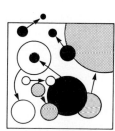 All of the above.
A word of caution: Please keep dot charts simple lest they become a tribute to Mickey Mouse or Star Wars.

There you have them, the five basic kinds of comparisons implied by the messages derived from the analysis of any data, and the chart forms most appropriate for demonstrating them.

To make sure you can apply the process in actual practice, test yourself with the two work projects that follow. Afterwards, review the shopping list of charts at work in Section 2 before placing the book on your bookshelf and referring to it whenever the need arises.

## WORK PROJECT A

Let's go back to the project we did at the end of Step B—identifying the comparison—and advance it to choosing the appropriate chart form for each of the 12 messages.

On the next pages are the 12 messages along with the kind of comparison you identified. Select the appropriate chart by referring to the matrix and sketch the chart you would use to support the respective messages.

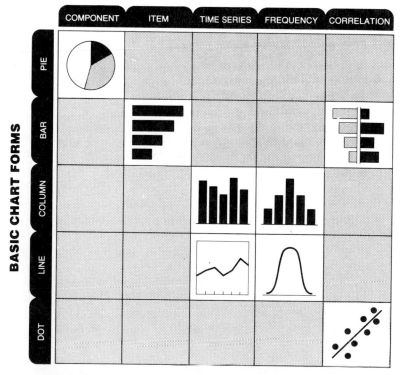

**KINDS OF COMPARISON**

As you sketch your charts, bear in mind the two important observations we've made.

1.  It's not the data or the measures that indicate which chart to use; it's what *you say* about it. For instance, you'll note that for Examples 4, 6, and 7, we want to show tenure measures, and yet, for each case, we have a different comparison implied, which leads to a different chart form. So focus your attention on the trigger words, the clues in your messages. In the solutions that follow the project, these words are underlined.

2.  Even without data, as we're doing here, you're able to decide which chart to use with the technique one of my colleagues called "visualizing the message, not the mess."

    The simplest test of whether a chart works is asking yourself about the finished chart: "Do I *see* what the message title *says?*" In other words, do the chart and the title work together; does the chart support the title; and does the title reinforce the chart? So, if I *say* in my title that "sales have increased significantly," I want to *see* a trend moving up at a sharp angle. If not, if the trend parallels the baseline, it's an instant clue the chart needs more thinking.

My solutions follow the messages. Don't worry if you've chosen a column chart and I show a line chart for time series comparisons or frequency distributions, or if you used the dot chart and I used a paired bar chart for correlations. In my solutions, the selection was arbitrary.

1. Sales are forecast to increase over the next 10 years
**Time Series**

2. The largest number of employees earns between $30,000 and $35,000
**Frequency Distribution**

3. Higher price of gasoline brands does not indicate better performance
**Correlation**

4. In September, the turnover rates for the six divisions were about the same
**Item**

5. The sales manager spends only 15% of his time in the field
**Component**

6. Size of merit increases is not related to tenure
**Correlation**

7. Last year, most turnover was in the 30 to 35 age group
   **Frequency Distribution**

8. Region C ranks last in productivity
   **Item**

9. Our company's earnings per share is declining
   **Time Series**

10. The largest share of total funds is allocated to manufacturing
    **Component**

11. There is a relationship between profitability and compensation
    **Correlation**

12. In August, two plants outproduced the other six by a wide margin
    **Item**

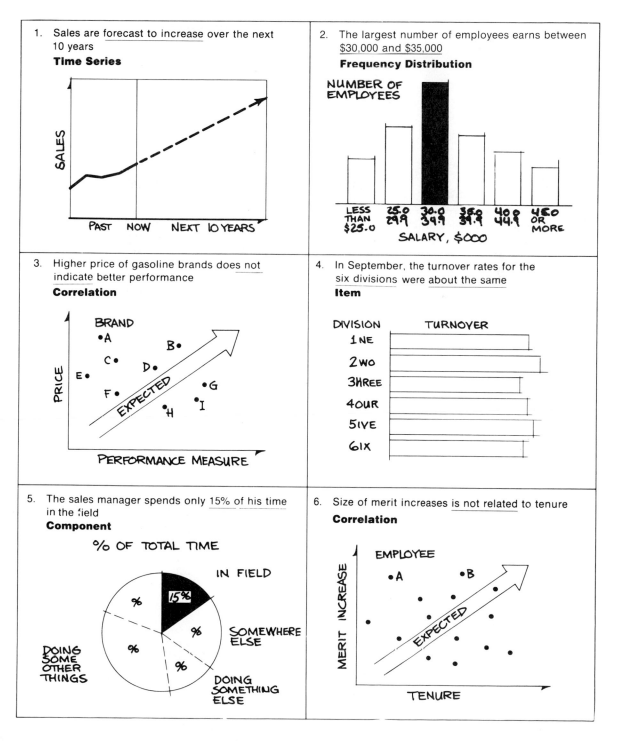

1. Sales are forecast to increase over the next 10 years
   **Time Series**

2. The largest number of employees earns between $30,000 and $35,000
   **Frequency Distribution**

3. Higher price of gasoline brands does not indicate better performance
   **Correlation**

4. In September, the turnover rates for the six divisions were about the same
   **Item**

5. The sales manager spends only 15% of his time in the field
   **Component**

6. Size of merit increases is not related to tenure
   **Correlation**

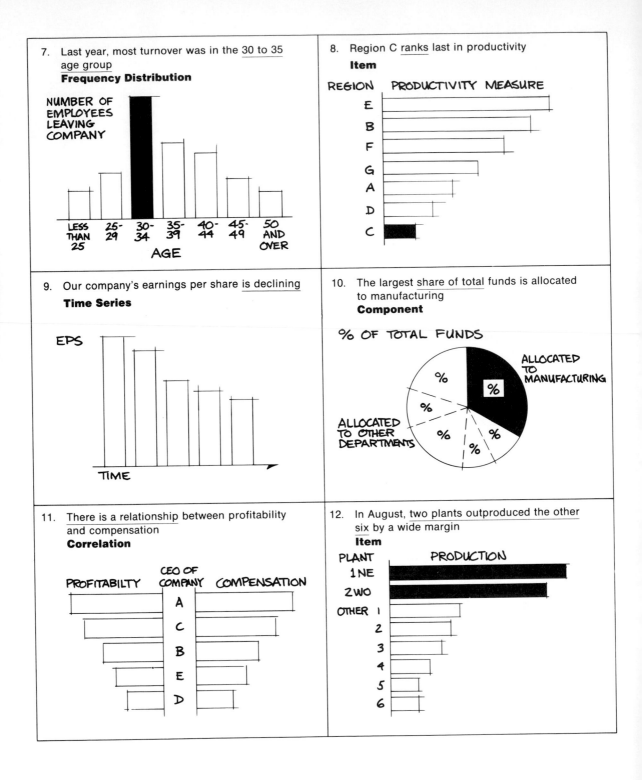

7. Last year, most turnover was in the 30 to 35 age group
**Frequency Distribution**

NUMBER OF EMPLOYEES LEAVING COMPANY

LESS THAN 25 | 25-29 | 30-34 | 35-39 | 40-44 | 45-49 | 50 AND OVER

AGE

8. Region C ranks last in productivity
**Item**

REGION — PRODUCTIVITY MEASURE

E
B
F
G
A
D
C

9. Our company's earnings per share is declining
**Time Series**

EPS

TIME

10. The largest share of total funds is allocated to manufacturing
**Component**

% OF TOTAL FUNDS

ALLOCATED TO MANUFACTURING

ALLOCATED TO OTHER DEPARTMENTS

%  %  %  %  %  %

11. There is a relationship between profitability and compensation
**Correlation**

PROFITABILTY | CEO OF COMPANY | COMPENSATION

A
C
B
E
D

12. In August, two plants outproduced the other six by a wide margin
**Item**

PLANT — PRODUCTION

1 NE
2 WO
OTHER 1
2
3
4
5
6

## WORK PROJECT B

Now, of course, in the business world we would go through the process *with* data, so let's apply the method to one last project using tabular information.

On the following pages, you'll find several sets of data drawn from an analysis of the imagin-a-toy industry. This industry manufactures mythical toys, including Slithy Toves, Gimbling Wabes, Mimsy Borogoves, Outgrabe Mome Raths, and the ever-popular Frumious Bandersnatch. The industry is made up of six competitors; ours is the Kryalot Company.

On the basis of the instructions given and the data presented, sketch the appropriate charts in the space provided. (The spaces have grids that are divided into 10 boxes to the inch to simplify plotting.)

In every instance, be sure to identify the kind of comparison the message implies and refer to the matrix to select the appropriate chart form. Also, write the message title you would use to reinforce the point each chart makes about our company.

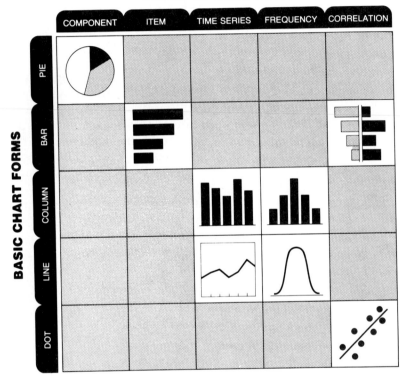

The solution for each problem is presented on the back.

# Exhibit 1

On the basis of the following data, sketch a chart to demonstrate Kryalot's share of imagin-a-toy industry sales in 1997 compared with that of our competitors'.

**Share of Industry Sales by Company, 1997**

| | |
|---|---|
| Kryalot | 19.3% |
| Competitor A | 10.1% |
| Competitor B | 16.6% |
| Competitor C | 12.4% |
| Competitor D | 31.8% |
| Competitor E | 9.8% |
| | 100.0% |

## SOLUTION

For Exhibit 1, the phrase "share of 1997 industry sales" serves as the clue to a component comparison—the size of the parts as a percentage of the total—and calls for a pie chart since we're speaking about a single total.

Here, the components have been arranged clockwise, proceeding from the company with the largest share to the company with the smallest, thereby positioning Kryalot as having the second-largest share. To emphasize Kryalot's share, we used the shading for that segment.

**Exhibit 1**

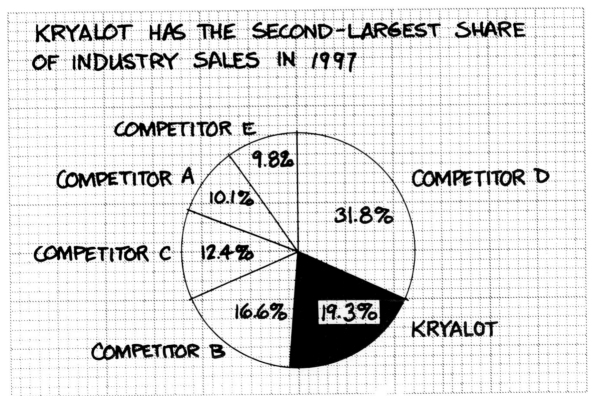

KRYALOT HAS THE SECOND-LARGEST SHARE OF INDUSTRY SALES IN 1997

COMPETITOR E — 9.8%
COMPETITOR A — 10.1%
COMPETITOR C — 12.4%
COMPETITOR D — 31.8%
16.6%
19.3% — KRYALOT
COMPETITOR B

# Exhibit 2

Sketch a chart that demonstrates how Kryalot's return on assets ranks in the industry in 1997.

**Return on Assets, 1997**

| | |
|---|---|
| Kryalot | 8.3% |
| Competitor A | 9.8% |
| Competitor B | 15.9% |
| Competitor C | 22.4% |
| Competitor D | 14.7% |
| Competitor E | 19.1% |

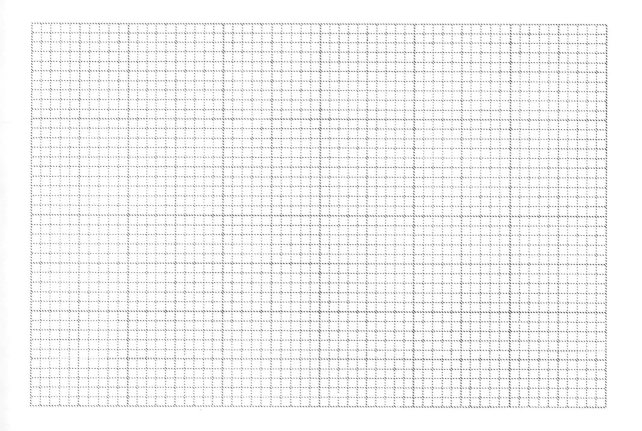

## SOLUTION

In Exhibit 2, the word "rank" is the trigger that implies an item comparison. Here, we want to know which competitor has the highest return on assets and which has the lowest. In this case, Kryalot has the lowest. Notice how the bar chart effectively demonstrates the point by positioning Kryalot at the bottom of the list and emphasizing it once more with the darkest shading.

**Exhibit 2**

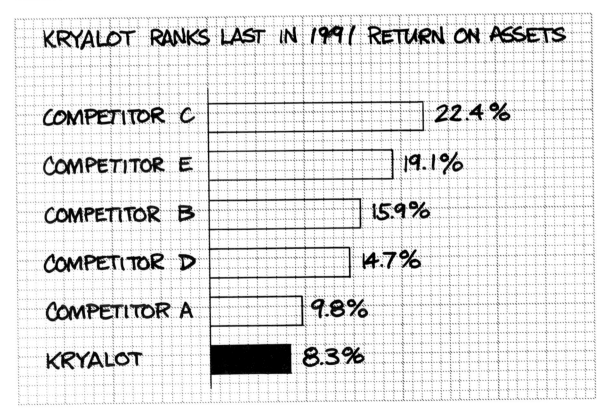

KRYALOT RANKS LAST IN 1991 RETURN ON ASSETS

| | |
|---|---|
| COMPETITOR C | 22.4% |
| COMPETITOR E | 19.1% |
| COMPETITOR B | 15.9% |
| COMPETITOR D | 14.7% |
| COMPETITOR A | 9.8% |
| KRYALOT | 8.3% |

# Exhibit 3

Sketch a chart that demonstrates whether a relationship exists between share of sales and return on assets in the imagin-a-toy industry in 1997.

## Share of Industry Sales, 1997

| | |
|---|---|
| Kryalot | 19.3% |
| Competitor A | 10.1% |
| Competitor B | 16.6% |
| Competitor C | 12.4% |
| Competitor D | 31.8% |
| Competitor E | 9.8% |

## Return on Assets, 1997

| | |
|---|---|
| Kryalot | 8.3% |
| Competitor A | 9.8% |
| Competitor B | 15.9% |
| Competitor C | 22.4% |
| Competitor D | 14.7% |
| Competitor E | 19.1% |

## SOLUTION

We would normally expect a relationship between share of sales and return on assets; that is, the greater the share, the higher the return. Here, the data indicate this is not so. For instance, although Kryalot has the second-largest share, it has a return much lower than that of, say, Competitor C, which ranks fourth in its share of market.

Although the dot chart would be equally appropriate, the paired bar chart allows us to label each set of paired bars more effectively.

**Exhibit 3**

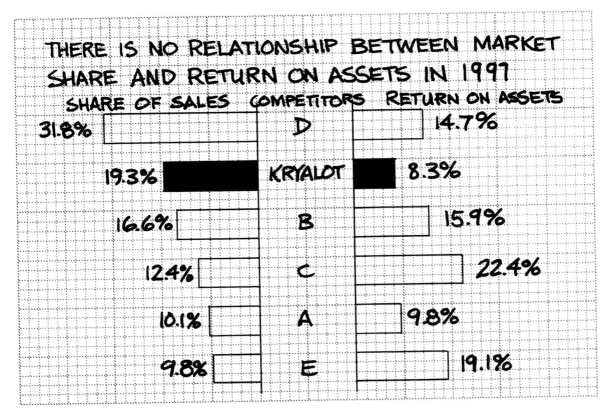

THERE IS NO RELATIONSHIP BETWEEN MARKET SHARE AND RETURN ON ASSETS IN 1997

| SHARE OF SALES | COMPETITORS | RETURN ON ASSETS |
|---|---|---|
| 31.8% | D | 14.7% |
| 19.3% | KRYALOT | 8.3% |
| 16.6% | B | 15.9% |
| 12.4% | C | 22.4% |
| 10.1% | A | 9.8% |
| 9.8% | E | 19.1% |

# Exhibit 4

Sketch a chart that demonstrates the trends for Kryalot's sales and earnings between 1993 and 1997, using 1993 as the base year and showing succeeding years as a percentage of the base year.

**Kryalot Net Sales**

|      | $ Millions | 1993 = 100 |
|------|------------|------------|
| 1993 | $387       | 100        |
| 1994 | 420        | 109        |
| 1995 | 477        | 123        |
| 1996 | 513        | 133        |
| 1997 | 530        | 137        |

**Kryalot Earnings**

|      | $ Millions | 1993 = 100 |
|------|------------|------------|
| 1993 | $24        | 100        |
| 1994 | 39         | 162        |
| 1995 | 35         | 146        |
| 1996 | 45         | 188        |
| 1997 | 29         | 121        |

## SOLUTION

Exhibit 4 calls for demonstrating changes over time—a time series comparison—and the line chart serves the purpose well.

We translated the absolute data into percentages of a best value—in this case 1993 figures—to provide a common, and clearer, basis for comparison of disparate figures: $530 million as compared to $29 million.

This is an excellent example of the value charts have over tabular data. The chart clearly demonstrates the erratic pattern of earnings, which might not have been as obvious had the data been left in tabular form.

**Exhibit 4**

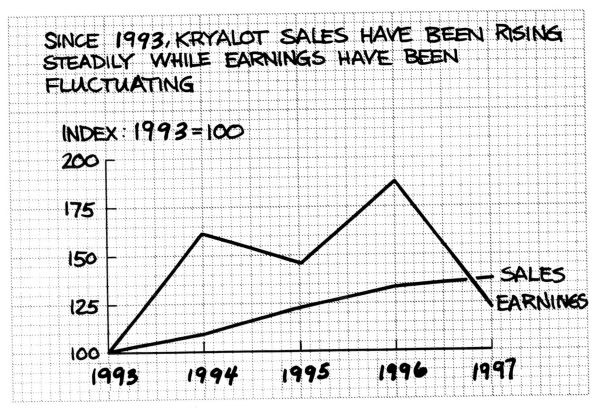

SINCE 1993, KRYALOT SALES HAVE BEEN RISING STEADILY WHILE EARNINGS HAVE BEEN FLUCTUATING

INDEX: 1993 = 100

## Exhibit 5

Sketch a chart demonstrating that in 1997 most of our sales, unlike those of Competitor D, are for the less expensive models for Frumious Bandersnatches.

**Number of Units Sold, 000**

| Size of Sales | Kryalot | Competitor D |
|---|---|---|
| Less than $5.00 | 320 | 280 |
| $ 5.00–$ 9.99 | 770 | 340 |
| $10.00–$14.99 | 410 | 615 |
| $15.00–$19.99 | 260 | 890 |
| $20.00 or more | 105 | 550 |

## SOLUTION

Exhibit 5 calls for a frequency distribution comparison, that is, the number of units that are sold in particular price ranges. In this case, we displayed the column chart for Kryalot against the stepped column chart for Competitor D. Two superimposed lines could also have been shown but, with so few data points, the columns are preferable.

**Exhibit 5**

# Exhibit 6

Sketch a chart that demonstrates how our product sales mix differs from that of Competitor D's in 1997.

**Percentage of Total Sales by Product, 1997**

| Products | Kryalot | Competitor D |
|---|---|---|
| Slithy Toves | 15.0% | 25.3% |
| Gimbling Wabes | 8.4% | 21.3% |
| Mimsy Borogoves | 20.6% | 19.9% |
| Outgrabe Mome Raths | 16.2% | 18.6% |
| Frumious Bandersnatches | 39.8% | 14.9% |
| | 100.0% | 100.0% |

## SOLUTION

In this last exhibit, we're back where we started with a component comparison—that is, showing percentage of total sales. As the matrix indicates, we could use pie charts. However, since we're dealing with more than one total, one for Kryalot *and* one for Competitor D, we're better off with 100 percent columns. This avoids the redundant labels that would have to be used with two pies, eliminates the need for a legend, and gives us a chart that more quickly demonstrates the relationships between the segments.

**Exhibit 6**

IN 1997, KRYALOT'S PRODUCT MIX DIFFERS
FROM THAT OF COMPETITOR D'S

| | KRYALOT 100% | COMPETITOR D 100% |
|---|---|---|
| GIMBLING WABES | 8.4% | 21.3% |
| SLITHY TOVES | 15.0% | |
| OUTGRABE MOME RATHS | 16.2% | 25.3% |
| MIMSY BOROGOVES | 20.6% | 18.6% |
| FRUMIOUS BANDERSNATCHES | 39.8% | 19.9% |
| | | 14.9% |

Let me summarize the major messages presented thus far.

¶ Charts are an important form of language. When well conceived and designed, they help you communicate more quickly and more clearly than you can with the data in tabular form.

¶ It's neither the data nor the measures that indicate what form of chart to use; it's *your* message, what *you* want to show, the specific point *you* want to make.

¶ Fewer is better. Use charts only when they will clearly help to get your message across.

¶ Charts are visual *aids;* they are not a substitute for writing or saying what you mean. Help them help you get your message across, and they'll serve you well.

*Section 2*

# USING CHARTS

**F**ollowing is a portfolio of 80 charts at work. The charts are organized around the five basic kinds of comparison: component, item, time series, frequency distribution, and correlation. The time series section is further subdivided into a segment each for column charts, line charts, and combinations of column and line charts. Within each section, the charts are presented in increasing order of complexity ranging from, say, one pie per chart to multiple pies.

Note: All charts in this book are derived from fictitious data. They are for illustrative purposes only and must not be used as source material for content.

## MESSAGE TITLES

To reinforce Step 1 in the process of choosing charts, *message titles* are included for all the examples. In actual practice, you might want to delete them from the charts. For example, when producing 35mm slides where space is limited, you might decide to include the message title only in your written script and not show it on the slide. However, omitting the title does not mean omitting the step of making certain, first and foremost, that *you* are clear about *your* message, what *you* want to show, the specific point *you* want to make, since this will determine the chart form to use.

## DUAL COMPARISONS

For some of the examples, you will note that the charts look suspiciously as if they should belong in another segment. This was done because, at times, the *message* you have determined, based upon your analysis of the data, will imply a *dual* comparison, e.g., item and component or time series and item. In these cases, you must determine which comparison is primary and which is secondary. Consider, for example, the following message which contains both a time series and an item comparison: "Sales are forecast to increase over the next 10 years, but profits may not keep pace." The first part of the message is a time series comparison. But with the statement, "but profits may not keep pace," we add a second, item, comparison. In other words, we are interested not only in the chronological change in sales (time series) but also in the performance of sales (item number 1) compared with profits (item number 2). However, the primary emphasis remains on changes over time, and we would therefore use the basic chart form most appropriate to a time series comparison. In this case, the best choice would be a line chart with a separate line for each of the two items. In the portfolio, these dual comparison charts have been included in the section on the comparison I judged to be primary.

## SCALES

Scale values have been omitted since the nature and magnitude of the data being plotted (e.g., sales dollars in thousands) is not important for our purposes in this portfolio. Naturally, scale values are used in practice, but omitting them should not obscure the relationship each chart illustrates. In fact, it is a good test of your own charts to see whether messages come across clearly without showing the scales.

This does not mean that scaling considerations are unimportant to the design of charts.[1] On the contrary, the wrong scale can lead to producing a chart that is misleading or worse, dishonest. Here is an extreme example of each.

[1] For a more thorough presentation of the misuse and abuse of scales, refer to my article, "Grappling with Graphics," *Management Review*, October 1975. The selected examples presented in this section are reprinted, with the permission of the publisher, from MANAGEMENT REVIEW, October 1975 © 1975 by AMACOM, a division of American Management Associations, New York. All rights reserved.

# EXAMPLE ▶ 1

**Misleading**                                                                     **Accurate**

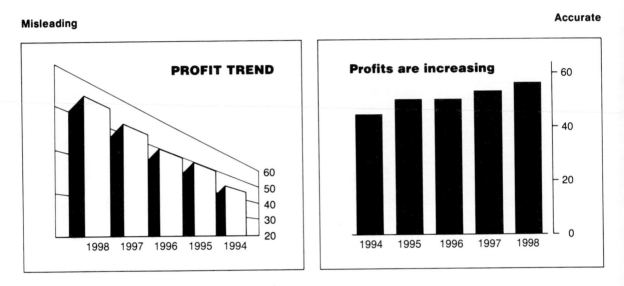

In Example 1, the chart at the left shows a picture of the trend in profits for the past five years. Our quick impression is that profits are declining. However, on closer inspection we notice four scaling problems: (1) the years are shown in reverse, moving from the most recent year at the left to earlier years at the right (a carry-over from annual reports, in which the most recent annual data are placed at the left to attract more immediate attention); (2) the bottom 20 units of profits are lopped off; (3) the columns are in three dimensions, so it's hard to know whether to measure their height from the front or the rear; (4) the scale lines are drawn in perspective. Together they create an unfortunately misleading picture of declining performance. Pity the shareholders.

In the chart at the right, we see more quickly and clearly that profits are increasing.

## EXAMPLE ▶ 2

**Dishonest**                                                                                                      **Accurate**

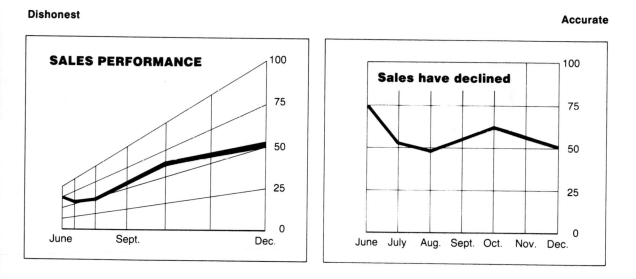

In the second example, foreshortening the scale lines in the chart on the left produces the impression that sales are increasing. Not true, as we can see from the chart on the right.

The point is this: a chart is a picture of relationships, and only the picture counts. Everything else—titles, labels, scale values—merely identifies and explains. The most important feature of the picture is the *impression* you receive. Scaling has an important controlling effect on that impression. Here is a demonstration of how easily and how substantially the scale can shape your impression of the message. Which would you choose, A or B?

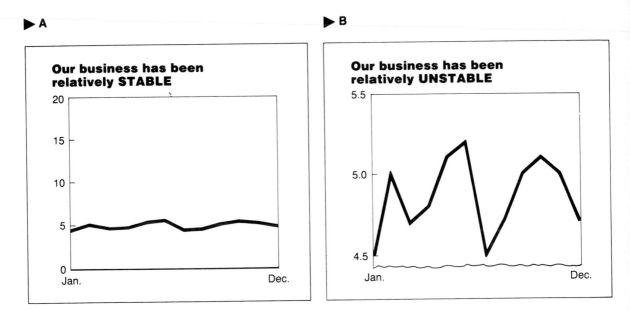

▶ A

**Our business has been relatively STABLE**

▶ B

**Our business has been relatively UNSTABLE**

It would be easy to opt for the answer: "Something in between," and yet that, too, may be inappropriate. The decision rests on *your professional understanding of the significance of the changes.* And so, a $1,000 change in a multimillion contract may be insignificant while a one-cent change in the price of a floor tile may be. You would therefore select a scale to reflect your understanding of the importance of the changes; perhaps the picture at the left would be appropriate for contracts, the one at the right for floor tiles.

To provide an accurate impression of your understanding of the changes, construct your charts with a respect for the factors that influence the picture:

The shape of the chart, from short and wide to tall and narrow

The scale range, say, 0 to 5, 0 to 10, or 0 to 25

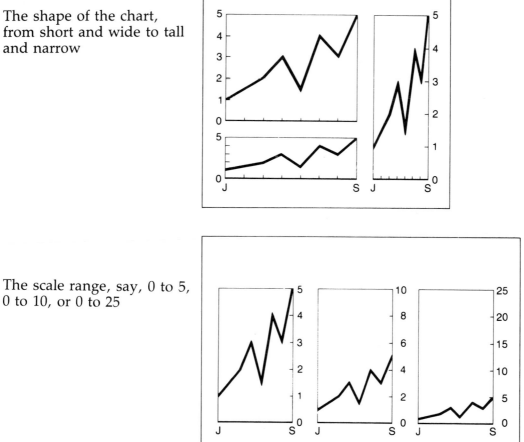

These and other important scaling considerations are discussed in the commentary that accompanies each chart in the portfolio.

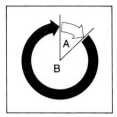

COMPONENT COMPARISON

*Shows the size of each part as
a percentage of the total*

# COMPONENT COMPARISON

▶ 1

Chart 1 illustrates the
simplest—and only truly
appropriate—use of the
pie chart: to compare a
few components. Four
shadings are used to
distinguish the companies,
with the darkest shading
reserved for Company A
to emphasize the aspect of
the data mentioned in the
title.

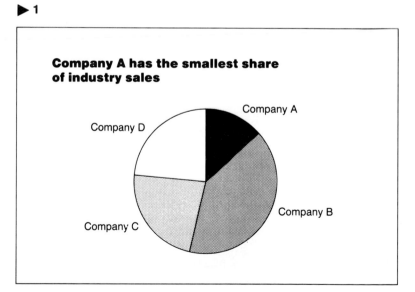

Chart 2 illustrates two methods of focusing attention on a component: (1) using darker shading; and (2) separating the segment from the remainder of the pie. In this example, the components are arranged according to the natural flow of activities.

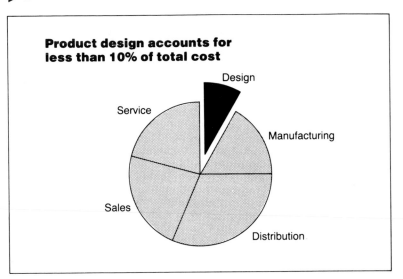

**Product design accounts for less than 10% of total cost**

Design

Service

Manufacturing

Sales

Distribution

Because the eye tends to complete the circumference of a circle, omitting a segment draws attention to the missing component, as Chart 3 shows. In this case, the lack of effort in recruiting new business is implied by the omission of the segment. The arrow further draws your attention to the sector.

**Agent's daily responsibilities leave little time for recruiting new business**

Traveling

Desk work

Open-debit collection

Office meetings

▶ 4

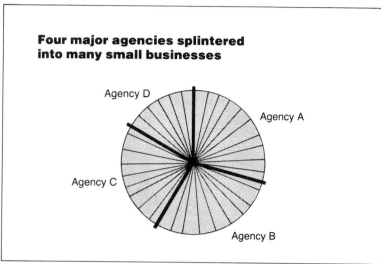

**Four major agencies splintered into many small businesses**

Agency D

Agency A

Agency C

Agency B

Although Chart 4 violates the guideline against using more than six components in a pie chart, it is used in this case to emphasize the message that there are many agency businesses. Note that it is virtually impossible to measure the relative size of each component; if you must do so, you are better off presenting the data in tabular form or as a bar chart (see Charts 12 and 13).

▶ 5

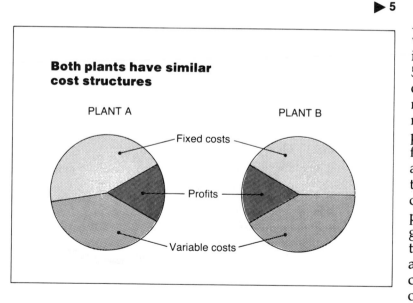

**Both plants have similar cost structures**

PLANT A

PLANT B

Fixed costs

Profits

Variable costs

Arranging the components within each pie in a mirror image, as is done in Chart 5, permits the use of only one set of labels. This makes it unnecessary to repeat the labels for each pie or to use a legend that forces you to look back and forth from the legend to the respective component. In the process, we disregard two guidelines: (1) starting at the 12 o'clock baseline; and (2) arranging the components in the same order.

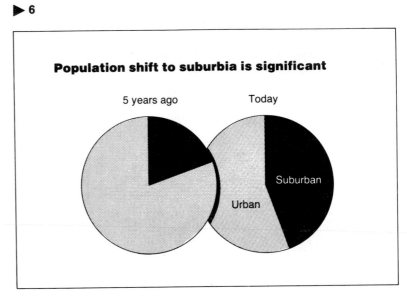

▶ 6

**Population shift to suburbia is significant**

5 years ago          Today

Suburban

Urban

Chart 6 compares components within separate pies. When using this technique, keep things simple—no more than three components, no more than two pies. Beyond two pies, it is better to switch to 100 percent columns (see Chart 40).

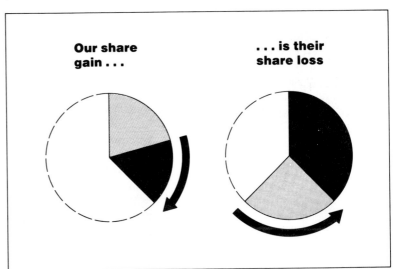

▶ 7

**Our share gain . . .**          **. . . is their share loss**

I hesitate to include Chart 7, since it will work only with two components, and even then the shading may be confusing. On the other hand, when kept simple, as we see here, it can be memorable. If in doubt, do not hesitate and use the more conventional two sets of 100 percent columns.

▶ 8

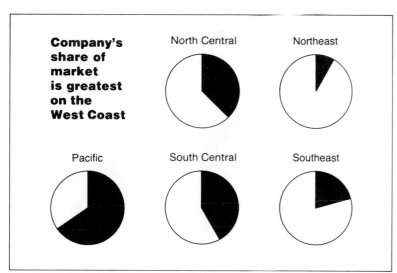

By using a separate pie for each region, as in Chart 8, we see: first, the company's share in each region; and second, the variation from region to region. Although 100 percent bars (see Chart 21) could be used, positioning the pies to simulate the natural geographic location makes this presentation more effective.

▶ 9

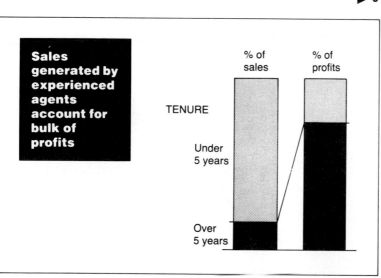

Chart 9 illustrates that, as soon as you need to show the relationship among components for more than one total, you are better off with either 100 percent bars or 100 percent columns. Commonly referred to as the 20/80 chart, this chart demonstrates that, although the more experienced agents account for the smallest share of sales, they concentrate on those sales that generate the larger share of profits.

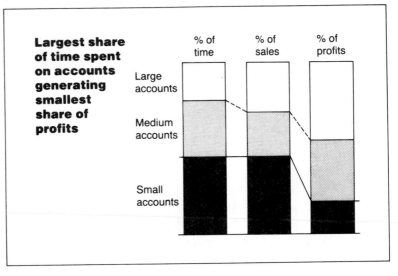

You can show more
than two items and two
components per item in a
100 percent column chart,
as Chart 10 indicates, but
you should avoid using
more than three of each
because it may become
confusing to follow this
kind of comparison.
Charts 9 and 10 could be
shown with horizontal
rather than vertical
bars. However, the
arrangements shown have
become widely used and
accepted.

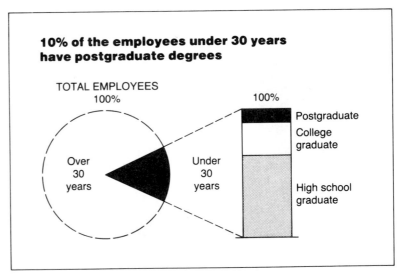

Chart 11 combines a pie
chart and a 100 percent
column to permit
comparison of a total
within a total: (1) of total
employees, the percentage
who are under 30 years
old; and (2) of those under
30, the percentage
distribution by education
level.

When using this
combination, always start
with the pie chart and
follow with the 100
percent column, not the
other way around.

86

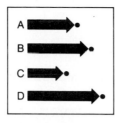

ITEM COMPARISON

*Shows ranking of items*

# ITEM COMPARISON

 **12**

In a bar chart, such as Chart 12, the order of the items can be important. In this presentation, the items are sequenced from high to low to provide a ranking from best to worst performance and to show where the client ranks in the lineup. The client's return on sales has been highlighted by using a darker shading and a different type style for the label.

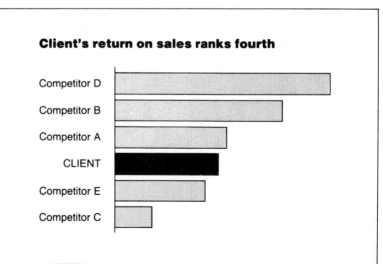

**Client's return on sales ranks fourth**

Instead of ranking the items from high to low or vice versa, Chart 13 uses a haphazard arrangement to emphasize the unevenness of salespersons' performance mentioned in the message title.

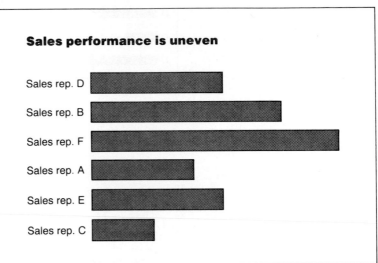

**Sales performance is uneven**

Sales rep. D

Sales rep. B

Sales rep. F

Sales rep. A

Sales rep. E

Sales rep. C

▶ 14

Chart 14 places the labels above instead of beside the bars. In this case, better use is made of the vertical space, permitting a smarter-looking and more compact layout. In the process, more space for the horizontal scale is provided to stress the important differences between departments.

**Turnover rates vary by department**

Research and Development

Manufacturing

Marketing

Distribution

▶ 15

**Two divisions suffered losses after cancellation of government contracts**

Division 3

Division 5

Division 1

Division 4

Division 6

Division 2

Chart 15 is a deviation bar chart in which bars extended to the left of the baseline—like columns extended below the zero line—suggest unfavorable results or conditions. The vertical baseline separates the profitable divisions from the losers. The items are ranked from most profitable to least profitable. To keep the chart compact, the labels are shifted from the left for profits to the right for losses.

▶ 16

**Range of discounts offered for the new model varies widely by area**

Smallest discount      Largest discount

Northeast

Southeast

North Central

South Central

Northwest

Southwest

Chart 16, a range bar chart, shows the spread between low and high amounts, rather than just the single amounts. Range bars are useful when interest is in the amounts at each end of the range as well as in the difference between them.

Chart 17 is a bar chart in which two or more sets of bars can be compared, providing for both vertical and horizontal comparison. Of the two comparisons, the vertical one is more direct because the items are measured against a common baseline, while it is more difficult to compare the items horizontally, since they do not stack against the same baseline. Although the averages could have been shown as bars, the dashed lines that cut across each company's performance distinguish more clearly those sales that are above the average from those that are below.

Chart 18 is a grouped bar chart that compares a number of items—Plants 1, 2, 3—at two points in time. Different shadings are used to distinguish time periods. The dashed lines and arrows, although not necessary, help to emphasize the direction and amount of change.

▶ 17

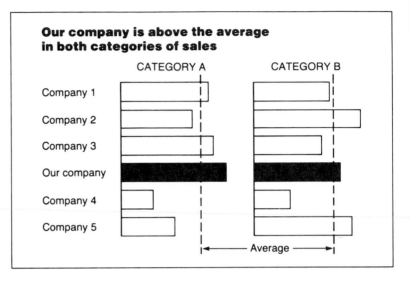

▶ 18

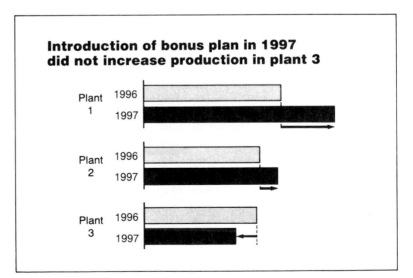

▶ 19

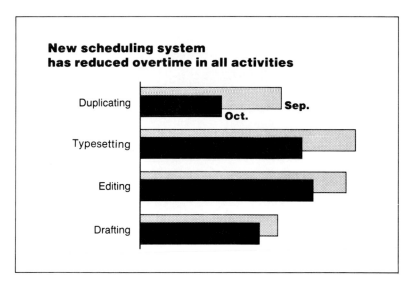

**New scheduling system
has reduced overtime in all activities**

Chart 19 is a special form of grouped bar chart that is sometimes effective. Overlapping the bars saves vertical space, helps to emphasize the more recent time period, and focuses attention on the gap between the two time periods. In this example, the activities are listed by the decreasing size of the gap. They could also have been arranged by the normal flow of activities, i.e., from editing to typesetting to drafting to duplicating. Note: this technique is effective only if the bar in the background is consistently longer than the one in the foreground. If it is not, the background bar appears thinner than the foreground bar and may confuse the viewer.

Charts 18 and 19 disregard the guideline against using bar charts to show changes over time. It works here with only two time periods. With more than two, use column charts.

Chart 20 is a subdivided bar chart in which the bars and their components are plotted according to absolute rather than relative values—that is, in dollars, tons, customers, or some other direct unit of measurement instead of in percentages.

Note that for all subdivided bar, column, and line charts, you should put the most important component against the baseline, since only the components against the base can be compared accurately.

Chart 21 is a 100 percent subdivided bar chart in which each bar and its components are plotted according to the relative (percentage) size of its components regardless of the absolute total value represented by the bar. In this type of chart, there are two baselines against which to place the important components—the one at the left, which connects the bars, and the one at the right, which is not connected.

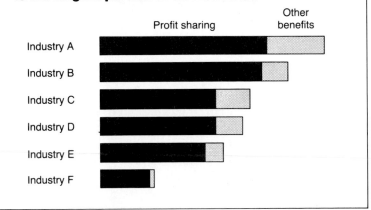

**Although total fringe benefits vary, profit sharing is the largest portion in all industries**

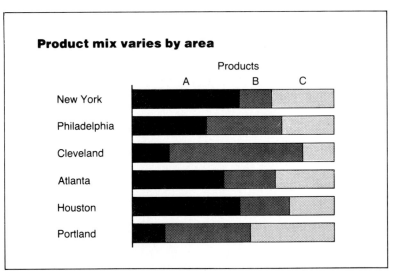

**Product mix varies by area**

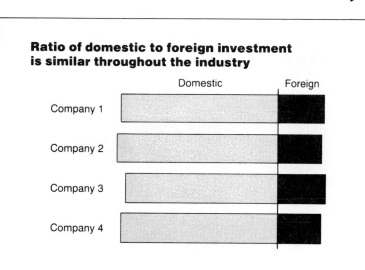

**► 22**

Chart 22 is a sliding subdivided bar chart, useful when there are only two components (or two major groups of components). Because the dividing line between the two segments serves as a common baseline, each component can be compared accurately. In this case the bars are 100 percent, although absolute values can also be used.

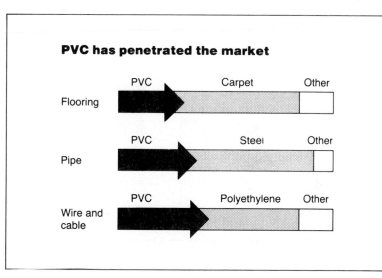

**► 23**

Charts 23 through 27 introduce the use of arrows in bar charts. Although not necessary, the arrows add a sense of direction and movement that can often add emphasis to the message title.

Chart 23 is, like Chart 21, a subdivided 100 percent bar chart. Here, however, the arrows used to show PVC's share accent the idea of penetration mentioned in the title.

**24**

Chart 24 can prove valuable for visualizing the highlights of a profit and loss statement. The components of assets are built up to their cumulative total and balanced against the components of liabilities. Certainly the bars could be vertical instead of horizontal, although the treatment used here provides more room to the left of the bars for labeling the components.

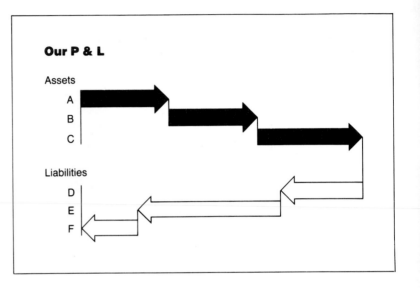

 **25**

Chart 25 has become known as a source of change chart. The solid arrows show the cost that is *added* at each successive stage of a process; the lighter segments indicate the carry-over from the previous stages.

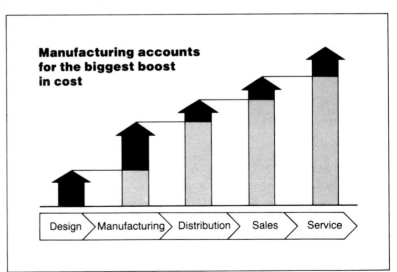

▶ 26

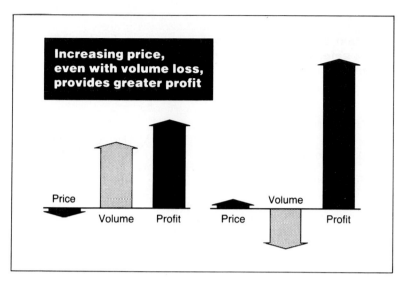

Sensitivity analyses are often demonstrated using the treatment shown in Chart 26. This deviation chart stresses the impact on profits of various changes in one or more related items. Here, use of dynamic arrows, rather than static bars, emphasizes the nature of the changes, both positive and negative.

▶ 27

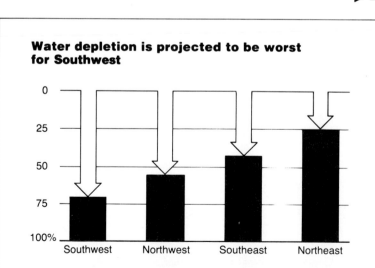

Chart 27 works well in spite of—or perhaps because of—the unconventional treatment of the scale, which begins at the top with 0 percent and moves down to 100 percent. The arrows stress the magnitude of the depletion while pointing to the percentage that remains. The items have been ranked beginning with the region most affected by the depletion and progressing to the region least affected.

▶ **28**

Chart 28 combines a pie chart, which summarizes the total picture, with a bar chart, which itemizes the reasons salespeople are leaving their current company. The solid bar focuses attention on the fact that most are leaving to take on similar positions with other companies, indicating a problem with their position in this company.

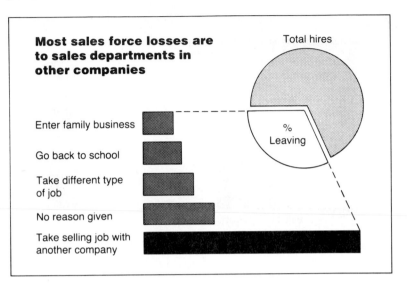

**Most sales force losses are to sales departments in other companies**

Total hires

%
Leaving

Enter family business

Go back to school

Take different type of job

No reason given

Take selling job with another company

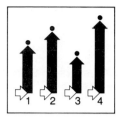

TIME SERIES COMPARISON

*Shows changes over time*

# TIME SERIES COMPARISON
## COLUMN CHARTS

▶ **29**

Chart 29 is a simple column chart suitable for showing changing levels over time. The column chart is best used for fewer than eight time periods.

Use graphic treatments—arrows, lines, shadings, or color—when you want to emphasize a specific aspect of the data, as shown here and on the next three charts. In this presentation, the arrow serves the dual purpose of focusing attention on the year 1996 and emphasizing the downward level.

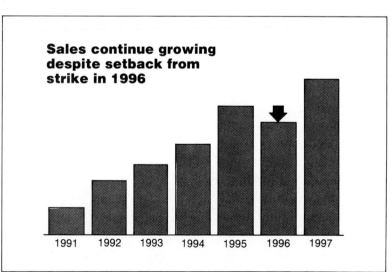

**Sales continue growing despite setback from strike in 1996**

**30**

In Chart 30, the arrow emphasizes the increase from 1991 through 1997.

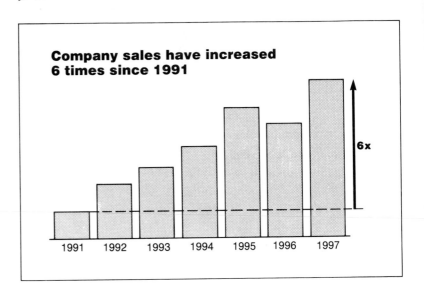

**Company sales have increased 6 times since 1991**

1991  1992  1993  1994  1995  1996  1997

6x

▶ **31**

Chart 31 uses lighter shading for 1996 to distinguish that year from all others. This treatment emphasizes how much sales *were* in 1996, rather than how much *less* they were than in 1995. This use of dark and light shading can also prove effective for distinguishing actual from estimated data or historical from projected data.

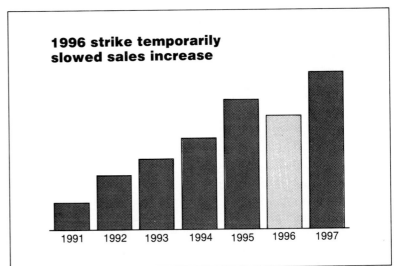

**1996 strike temporarily slowed sales increase**

1991  1992  1993  1994  1995  1996  1997

▶ 32

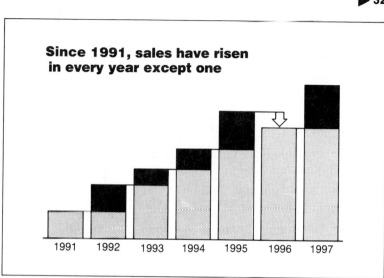

**Since 1991, sales have risen in every year except one**

1991  1992  1993  1994  1995  1996  1997

Chart 32 combines graphic treatments—darker column caps and an arrow—to highlight the amount of change from year to year and to distinguish between periods of growth and the period of decline.

▶ 33

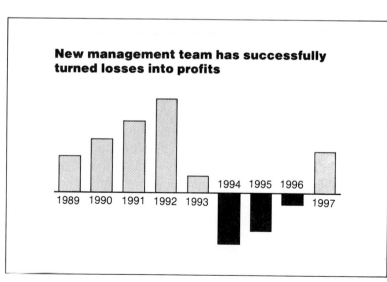

**New management team has successfully turned losses into profits**

1989  1990  1991  1992  1993  1994  1995  1996  1997

Chart 33 employs several techniques to distinguish between positive and negative data: (1) extending columns below the zero line to indicate deficits or unfavorable conditions; (2) using different shadings; and (3) staggering the column labels.

Chart 34 is on the page of our daily newspaper when we study the performance of the stock market. It is a range column chart and emphasizes the spread between two sets of values—in this case, the daily high and low—rather than just the magnitude of the values. The crossline, generally used to indicate the average of the high/low values, here indicates the closing level for each day.

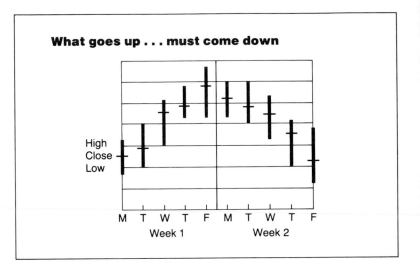

Chart 35 butts two column charts on either side of the baseline: above, the columns indicate the increasing number of rigs; below, they show the average depth the rigs drill into the earth. In this case, the columns extended below the line indicate neither a deficit nor an unfavorable condition, but instead reinforce the idea of depth; also, the columns have been narrowed to suggest drilling bits.

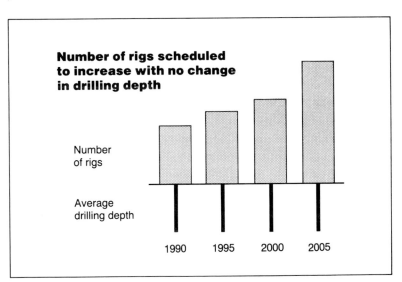

▶ **36**

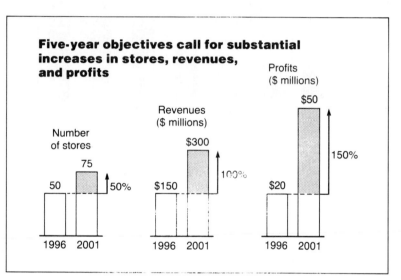

**Five-year objectives call for substantial increases in stores, revenues, and profits**

Number of stores

50   75   ↕50%

1996   2001

Revenues ($ millions)

$150   $300   ↕100%

1996   2001

Profits ($ millions)

$20   $50   ↕150%

1996   2001

Chart 36 is a grouped column chart for three sets of data that are measured in different kinds of units (number of stores versus dollars) and in different sized units (revenues in $ hundred millions versus profits in $ ten millions). To provide a common base of comparison, translate the absolute data into percentages (or an index) of the base value (in this case, 2001 divided by 1996) and plot the 1996 base values at equal heights. In other words, we assume that in 1996 the number of stores equaled the revenues and the profits. Then plot the 2001 values according to their percentage increase. The result is a "visual" index chart that allows you to show the absolute values while plotting the percentage changes in proportion to one another.

▶ 37

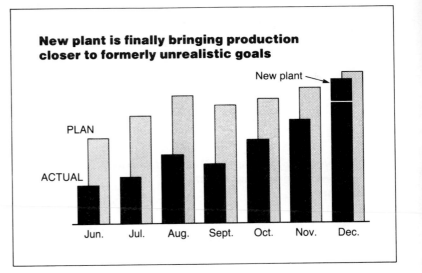

**New plant is finally bringing production closer to formerly unrealistic goals**

Overlapping columns, as in Chart 37, works well when the two items are related aspects of the same measurement. In this case, the two items—planned versus actual—are related aspects of production. (Remember, one item should be consistently greater than the other. Otherwise the overlapping column hides the thickness of the column in the background.)

▶ 38

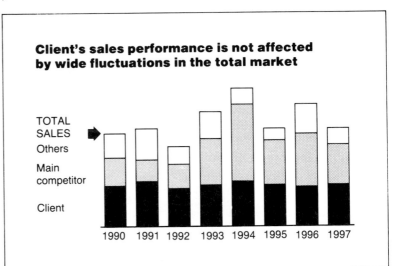

**Client's sales performance is not affected by wide fluctuations in the total market**

Chart 38 is a subdivided column chart that shows how the totals change over time and the components contribute to the change. For all subdivided charts, the tendency is to show too many components, making individual segments difficult to identify and compare. Use not more than five. If you need accurate measurements of each component, rely on the approach illustrated by the next chart.

▶ 39

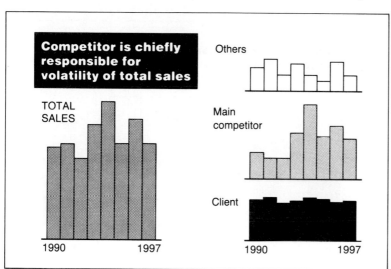

Chart 39 employs the same data used in Chart 38 but presents them in such a way that the trends for the total and for each component can be measured accurately against its own baseline. This alters the focus of the chart from how the components contribute to the changing trend over time to how each item varies over time.

▶ 40

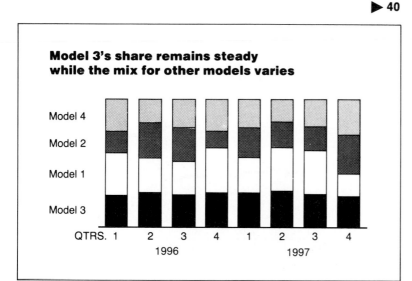

Chart 40 is a 100 percent subdivided column chart. Although the eye is accustomed to reading a page from top to bottom, a column chart is measured from the zero line up (as is a subdivided surface chart). For this reason, the most important component is usually positioned against that base. Use different shadings to distinguish the components within the columns and to help identify the pattern of change for each component across the chart.

▶ 41

Chart 41 is a column chart that indicates the source of change from the volume at the beginning of the time period to the volume at the end. Here, arrows reinforce the positive and negative nature of the changes while measuring the amounts of change each account represents.

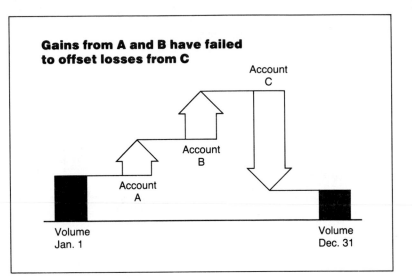

**Gains from A and B have failed to offset losses from C**

Account C

Account B

Account A

Volume
Jan. 1

Volume
Dec. 31

▶ 42

Chart 42, a step-column chart, could be thought of as a column chart with no space between the columns or as a surface (line) chart with the space between the line and the base shaded; without the shading, it becomes a line chart. It is best for presentation of data that change abruptly at irregular intervals, such as staffing levels.

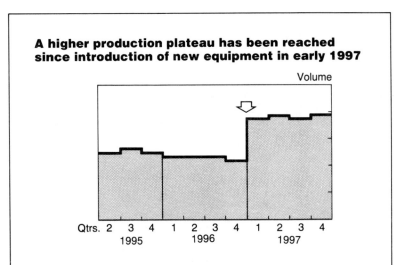

**A higher production plateau has been reached since introduction of new equipment in early 1997**

Volume

Qtrs.  2   3   4 | 1   2   3   4 | 1   2   3   4
    1995    |    1996    |    1997

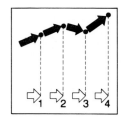

TIME SERIES COMPARISON

*Shows changes over time*

# TIME SERIES COMPARISON
## LINE CHARTS

▶ **43**

Chart 43 is a simple line chart that shows changes over time when you have many periods. Two graphic treatments are used: (1) the solid line for the actual is distinguished from the dashed line for the forecast; and (2) the arrows emphasize the direction and amount of change.

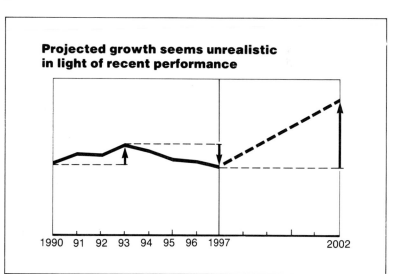

**Projected growth seems unrealistic in light of recent performance**

1990  91  92  93  94  95  96  1997  2002

**44**

Charts 44 through 53 are examples of grouped or multiple line charts.

As Chart 44 shows, when lines cross, use different patterns (e.g., dotted, dashed, solid, thick, thin) to eliminate confusion; when lines do not cross, this is not necessary. In any case, the bolder, solid line should be reserved for the most significant item.

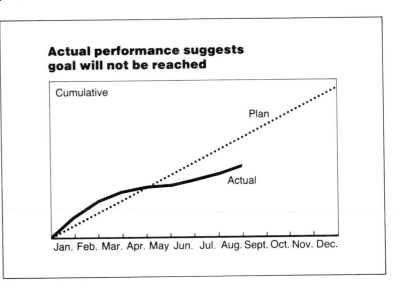

**Actual performance suggests goal will not be reached**

Cumulative

Plan

Actual

Jan. Feb. Mar. Apr. May Jun. Jul. Aug. Sept. Oct. Nov. Dec.

 **45**

The wavy line at the base of Chart 45 indicates that the bottom of the vertical scale has been cut. In this case, the focus is not on the relative levels of revenue versus expenditures (in that event, the chart should be plotted from the zero line) but on the differences between the two. Here, different shadings are used to distinguish surplus from deficit.

**Deficits continue to grow**

Revenue

Surplus

Deficit

Expenditures

1989    1992    1997

▶ 46

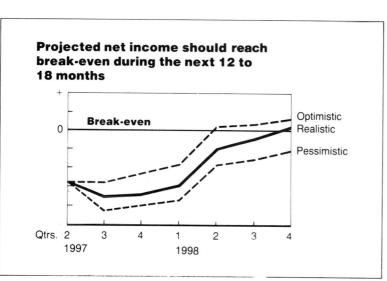

**Projected net income should reach break-even during the next 12 to 18 months**

Break-even

Optimistic
Realistic

Pessimistic

Qtrs. 2    3    4    1    2    3    4
     1997              1998

Chart 46 provides a cushion of safety when showing projected data. Establishing an optimistic/pessimistic range around the best-guess (realistic) trend line reduces the risk of being held accountable for a projection that is tenuous at best, no matter what the assumptions are. In this case, thin dashed lines are used to establish the range; shading the range would also work.

▶ 47

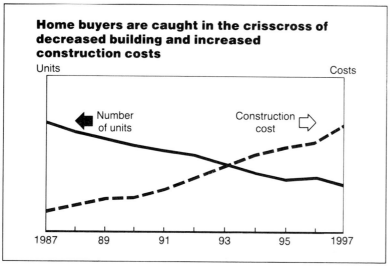

**Home buyers are caught in the crisscross of decreased building and increased construction costs**

Units                                    Costs

Number
of units

Construction
cost

1987    89    91    93    95    1997

Chart 47 is a multiple scale chart (i.e., different scales to the left and right), which brings together for close comparison two or more curves that are measured either in different units or are so far apart in size that they would be difficult to compare. If you wish to compare change or growth, make the zero lines of both scales coincide and select the scale intervals so that both curves meet at some meaningful point. Better still, convert both series to a common base (e.g., index numbers or percentage changes) and use only one scale.

Chart 48, plotted against a logarithmic (semilog) scale, shows the rate of change from any point to any other point in a series of data. On this kind of chart, absolute figures increasing at a constant rate (e.g., 5 percent each week) would be shown as a straight line; on an arithmetic scale chart, absolute figures increasing at a constant 5 percent rate would appear as a curving line slanting up at a steeper and steeper angle.

Since there is no zero line, this chart should not be used to measure levels, magnitudes, or negative data. It cannot legitimately be shown as a surface chart (or a column chart). Always use logarithmic scales with caution; if there is any chance that the reader may not understand the scale, explain how to read it and what to look for.

▶ 48

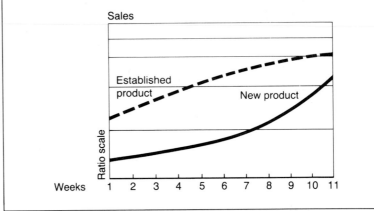

**As expected, new product sales are increasing faster than established products' sales**

▶ **49**

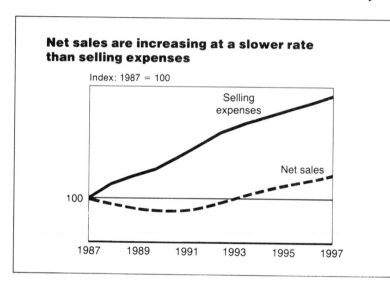

**Net sales are increasing at a slower rate than selling expenses**

Index: 1987 = 100

Selling expenses

Net sales

100

1987  1989  1991  1993  1995  1997

Chart 49 is an index scale chart, which shows data that have been converted into percentages of a base value. Unlike the logarithmic scale chart, which shows the relative change between *any* two points in time, the index scale chart shows the relative change only from the base value for each period. It offers an advantage over absolute amount scales since it can be used for comparing two or more series of data that are measured in different kinds of units or in different-sized units. This kind of comparison may be clearer if changes are presented as simple percentage differences. For example, "Percentage increase in sales since 1987" shows exactly the same picture as "Index of sales: 1987 = 100," except that in the former the scale is divided to read 0, 25 percent, 50 percent, instead of 100, 125, 150.

▶ **50**

Instead of index values, Chart 50 uses a scale that shows percentage changes between 1992 and 1997. To provide meaningful comparison between the three items—income, assets, and sales—the scales must be the same for all three. An option here is to show only two charts, one for Company A and one for Company B, and to plot each company's percentage change in income, assets, and sales on its own grid.

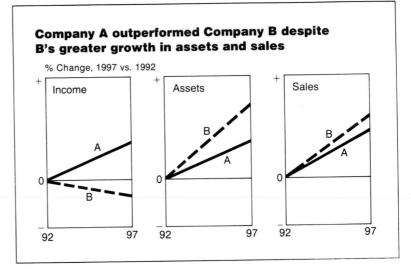

**Company A outperformed Company B despite B's greater growth in assets and sales**

% Change, 1997 vs. 1992

▶ **51**

Chart 51 uses a calculation tree to visualize a mathematical formula—in this case, return on investment equals return on sales multiplied by investment turnover. In each window, the trend for two companies is shown, allowing the reader to study the various branches of the tree for the source of any problem in the resulting ROI performance.

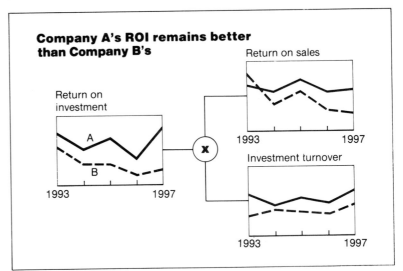

**Company A's ROI remains better than Company B's**

▶ 52

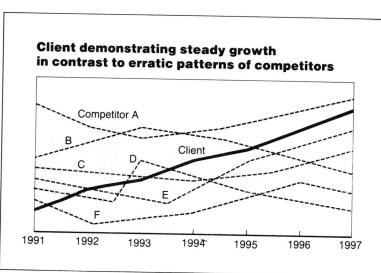

In Chart 52, the line representing the client is emphasized as a bold solid line and is compared to the lines for *all* competitors. If, on the other hand, you want to compare the client to *each* competitor, the technique in the next example is more appropriate.

▶ 53

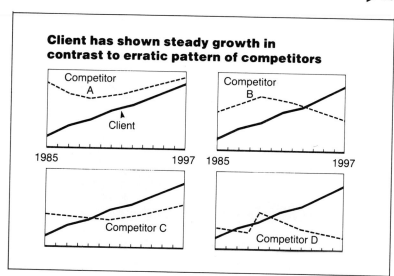

Chart 53 contains more charts (and therefore requires more drafting time) since it compares the client separately to each competitor, but the comparison per chart is simpler than in the previous example. The client line is identical on each chart. Using this approach, you can group the comparisons for easy reading (e.g., by competitors who were ahead, about the same, or behind the client at a given point in time). You might also emphasize client performance by using a surface chart rather than a curve.

54

Chart 54 is a surface chart, a line chart with the space between the trend line and the baseline shaded to give a greater feeling for quantity. The graphic treatment in this example—darker shading for the periods of decline—calls attention to the two quarters under scrutiny.

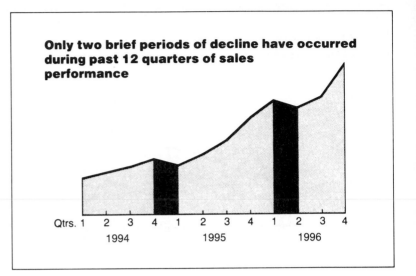

**Only two brief periods of decline have occurred during past 12 quarters of sales performance**

Qtrs. 1  2  3  4  1  2  3  4  1  2  3  4
        1994          1995          1996

▶ 55

Chart 55 demonstrates the change in the absolute contribution of three components over time, but with the primary emphasis on the total. Only the bottom layer is measured directly from a fixed base. All other layers are measured from a changing base, and their size can be gauged only approximately. To permit direct reading, use the approach illustrated by Chart 39. If the layers fluctuate sharply, use a subdivided column chart (see Chart 38) or the approach illustrated by Chart 39.

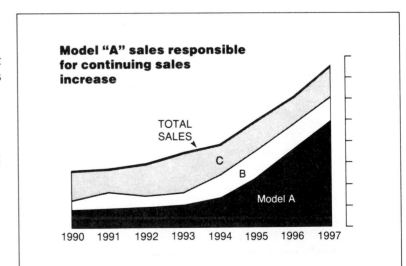

**Model "A" sales responsible for continuing sales increase**

TOTAL SALES

C

B

Model A

1990  1991  1992  1993  1994  1995  1996  1997

112

▶ **56**

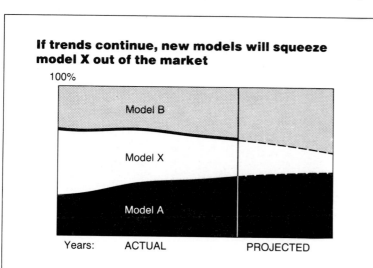

**If trends continue, new models will squeeze model X out of the market**

100%

Model B

Model X

Model A

Years: ACTUAL PROJECTED

Chart 56 shows the change in the relative contributions of components over time. The important component—in this case, Model X share—is sandwiched between the two competing models to stress the message. Like all charts illustrating relationships, this type of chart can be misleading if the percentages are based on absolute amounts that are not fairly stable. For example, if 100 percent represents a sharply rising total, a decreasing percentage may actually represent an increasing amount. In such cases, there is a special advantage in picturing the absolute amounts in an accompanying chart or table.

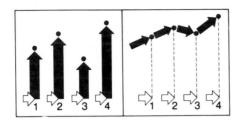

# TIME SERIES COMPARISON
## COMBINATION CHARTS

Charts 57 through 63 combine column and line charts to provide additional perspectives on changes over time.

Chart 57 could use grouped columns (that is, one column for capacity and another for orders) but, since capacity is constant, it is shown instead as a background line/surface chart. To emphasize the difference between capacity and orders—instead of their levels, as in this example—an option is to use a deviation chart (see Chart 33) with capacity as the baseline and measuring the number of orders below or above capacity.

▶ 57

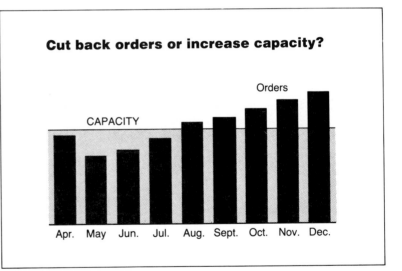

**Cut back orders or increase capacity?**

Orders

CAPACITY

Apr.  May  Jun.  Jul.  Aug.  Sept.  Oct.  Nov.  Dec.

▶ 58

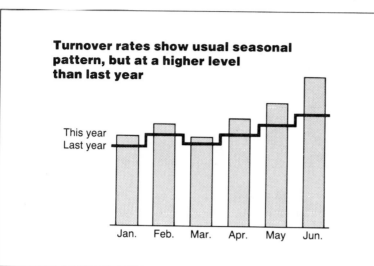

**Turnover rates show usual seasonal pattern, but at a higher level than last year**

This year
Last year

Jan.   Feb.   Mar.   Apr.   May   Jun.

Chart 58, too, could be presented as grouped columns (one column for this year, one for last year). On the other hand, this column and line technique places primary emphasis on the columns representing this year's activity and secondary emphasis on the comparison of this year's versus last year's data.

▶ 59

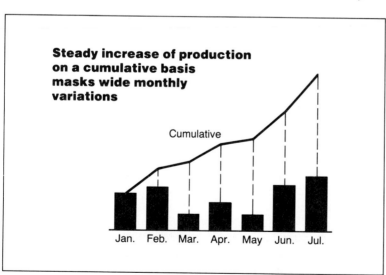

**Steady increase of production on a cumulative basis masks wide monthly variations**

Cumulative

Jan.   Feb.   Mar.   Apr.   May   Jun.   Jul.

Chart 59 combines a column chart to show the fluctuation in monthly production with a line chart to show the cumulative (sometimes referred to as year-to-date) trend since January.

**60**

Chart 60 uses a deviation column chart to show how the initial investments in 1992 and 1993 turn positive in 1994, and a line chart to indicate when the break-even point is achieved.

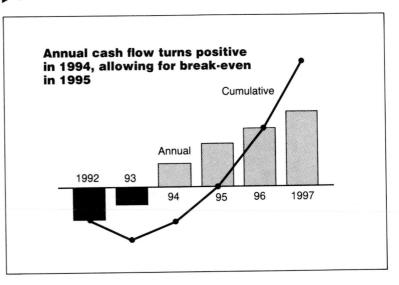

**Annual cash flow turns positive in 1994, allowing for break-even in 1995**

 **61**

Chart 61 is similar to Charts 59 and 60 but, in this case, the line represents the net difference between the gains and losses for each month rather than the cumulative trend.

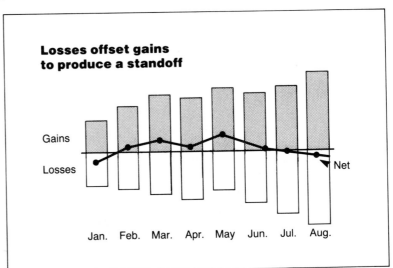

**Losses offset gains to produce a standoff**

▶ **62**

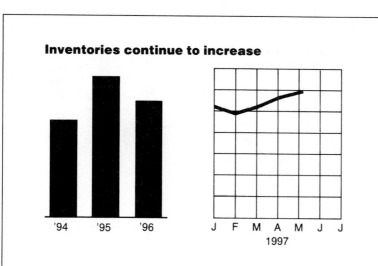

Chart 62 uses columns to summarize past annual data and a line chart to study this year's performance on a month-by-month basis. This technique is often used in management information systems; it leaves space to add monthly performance data, thereby eliminating the need to prepare a new chart each month.

▶ **63**

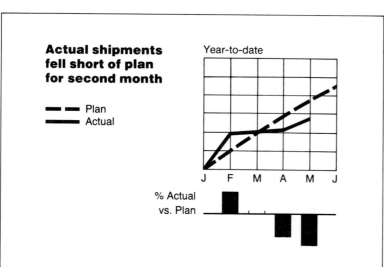

Chart 63 is also often seen in management information systems. It is a plot of actual monthly (or weekly or quarterly) results against the plan set at the beginning of the year (or against an objective or last year's total). On a cumulative basis, the differences between actual and plan usually tend to be small and often fail to focus attention on problem periods. To magnify these differences, it is a good idea to show the percentage variations of actual versus plan, as illustrated in this example.

Chart 64 combines pie charts with a line chart. The pies show the share mix at each point in time, and the line chart shows the changing totals over time. Keep it simple—not more than three components per pie, not more than one trend line, not more than six periods of time.

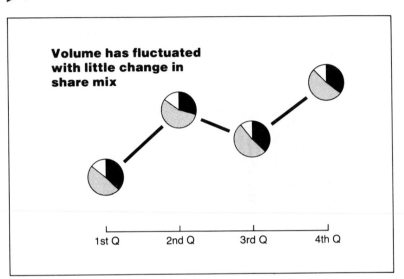

**Volume has fluctuated with little change in share mix**

1st Q     2nd Q     3rd Q     4th Q

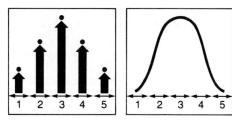

## FREQUENCY DISTRIBUTION COMPARISON

*Shows how many items fall into a series of progressive numerical ranges*

## FREQUENCY DISTRIBUTION COMPARISON

▶ 65

Chart 65 shows the histogram form of frequency distribution. Note that the ranges across the horizontal scale are equal and discrete.

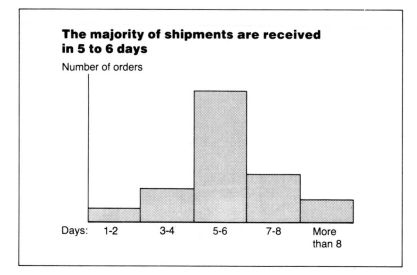

**The majority of shipments are received in 5 to 6 days**

Number of orders

Days: 1-2   3-4   5-6   7-8   More than 8

For continuous data—instead of discrete data as in Chart 65—use the histograph approach shown in Chart 66. Here, the horizontal scale shows the values lined up against the ticks rather than expressed as groups.

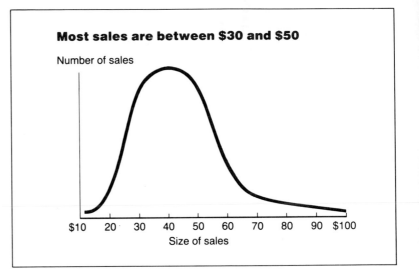

**Most sales are between $30 and $50**

Number of sales

$10   20   30   40   50   60   70   80   90   $100

Size of sales

Chart 67 combines the step column and step line to compare two distributions in the same chart.

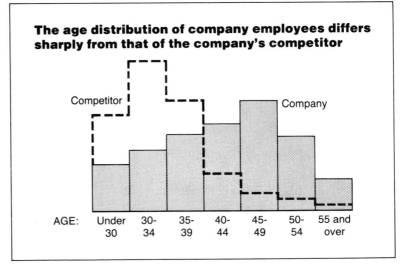

**The age distribution of company employees differs sharply from that of the company's competitor**

Competitor          Company

AGE:   Under   30-    35-    40-    45-    50-    55 and
        30     34     39     44     49     54     over

▶ 68

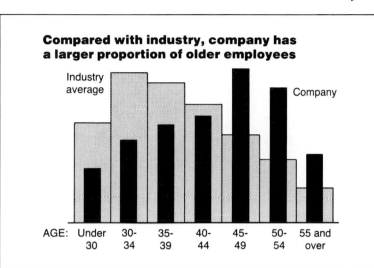

**Compared with industry, company has a larger proportion of older employees**

Industry average

Company

AGE: Under 30 | 30-34 | 35-39 | 40-44 | 45-49 | 50-54 | 55 and over

Chart 68 combines a column chart for company data and a step-column chart for the industry. This sort of treatment is especially appropriate for this kind of one-against-all comparison. In this case, some of the overlapping columns are bigger than the background columns without creating confusion (see discussion of Charts 19 and 37).

▶ 69

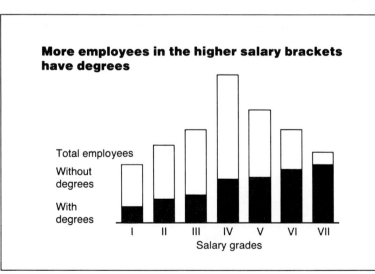

**More employees in the higher salary brackets have degrees**

Total employees

Without degrees

With degrees

I | II | III | IV | V | VI | VII
Salary grades

Chart 69 is a subdivided histogram that shows, primarily, the distribution of the total number of employees and, secondarily, the components of each salary grade. Here, the salary grade is a shortcut to showing the actual salary ranges.

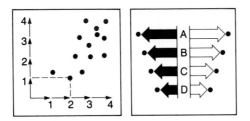

## CORRELATION COMPARISON

*Shows whether or not the relationship between two variables is as expected*

Chart 70 is a dot chart (scatter diagram), which helps determine whether the relationship between two variables follows an expected pattern. In this example, it would be expected that the greater the discount offered, the greater the volume sold. The arrow indicates where the expected pattern might fall and highlights the fact that the expected and actual patterns differ widely. Although the dots represent individual transactions, they do not specifically identify the salespersons, since labeling each dot would clutter the chart. An option for identifying specific salespeople is suggested in the following chart.

## CORRELATION COMPARISON

▶ 70

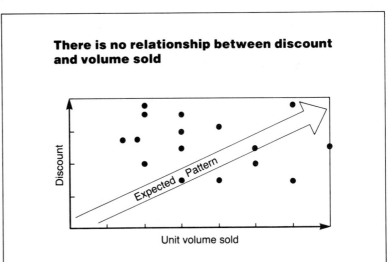

**There is no relationship between discount and volume sold**

Discount

Expected Pattern

Unit volume sold

► 71

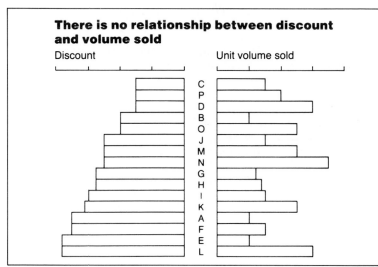

**There is no relationship between discount and volume sold**

Discount          Unit volume sold

C P D B O J M N G H I K A F E L

Chart 71 is a paired bar chart that lets you identify each transaction as well as see the overall correlation. Using the same data as in the previous chart, it ranks the items by size of discount. If the correlation ran as normally expected, the volume bars would mirror the pattern of discounts.

► 72

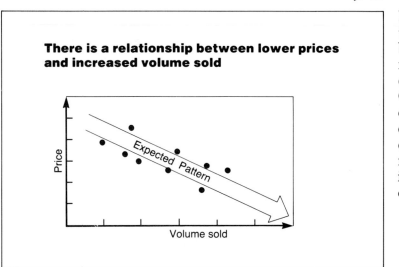

**There is a relationship between lower prices and increased volume sold**

Price

Expected Pattern

Volume sold

Depending upon the data, the expected pattern could be horizontal (indicating no relationship) or downward, as shown in Chart 72. Here, the dots cluster around the expected pattern pointing out that there *is* a relationship between increasing prices and declining volume sold.

Chart 73 uses the same data used in Chart 72, but presents them as a paired bar chart. In this example, the bars do not form a mirror image, but instead show a consistent pattern between prices and volume sold.

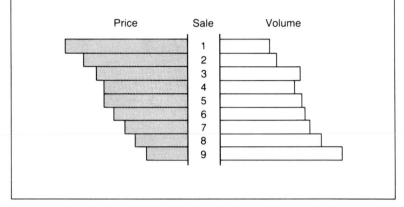

**There is a relationship between lower prices and increased volume sold**

Price    Sale    Volume

1
2
3
4
5
6
7
8
9

Chart 74 is a grouped dot chart that shows more than one item. To make the distinction between the two items, the chart uses dots and circles; other symbols, such as squares and triangles, can also be used.

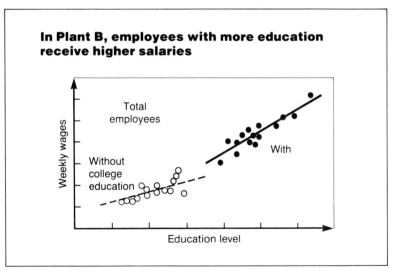

**In Plant B, employees with more education receive higher salaries**

Weekly wages

Total employees

Without college education

With

Education level

▶ 75

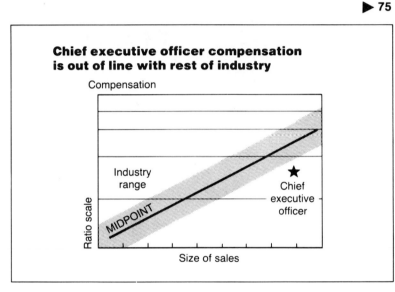

**Chief executive officer compensation is out of line with rest of industry**

Compensation

Industry range

Chief executive officer

MIDPOINT

Ratio scale

Size of sales

Chart 75 shows a correlation comparison using semilogarithmic scale. The two items in this example are the industry range (perhaps 5 percent above and below the midpoint) and the chief executive officer's compensation relative to his company's sales (shown by the star, the equivalent of a dot). On an arithmetic scale, the industry range would become larger as it moved across the chart, since it is usually computed as a constant percentage increase; it would also curve upward, making it difficult to study the relationships. This scale arrangement clarifies the comparison by "straightening out" the industry relationship and maintaining the range at a visually constant width.

Chart 76 is similar to Chart 75 except that the range is defined by the maximum, midpoint, and minimum of each salary grade. The dots represent the actual salaries of the employees in each grade and their relation to the range. The reason for reevaluating the structure is that most employees are above the midpoint of their range and many are above the maximum.

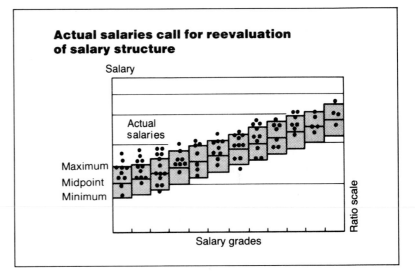

Chart 77 is a break-even chart that combines a subdivided surface chart to show costs (fixed and variable) with a line chart to show volume of sales. Although it appears out of place here among the dot charts and paired bar charts, it is used to show the correlation between increasing volume and higher cost. The vertical bar at the right can be added to identify the components of costs at a specific volume of sales.

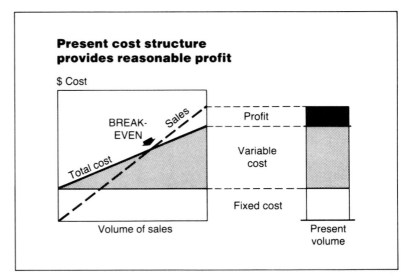

Chart 78 is also known as the "bubble chart." It is little more than a dot chart in which dots of differing sizes reflect a third dimension. In this example of a company's business portfolio, each of nine businesses is positioned according to the correlation of market attractiveness and company strength; the farther into the upper right-hand corner, the better the business. The dot representing each business is enlarged into a "bubble" to indicate, in this case, the range of profits contributed by that business.

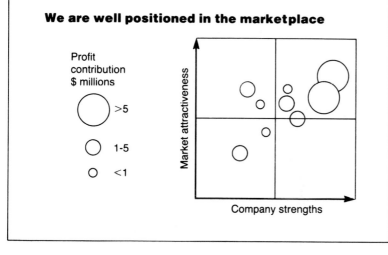

Chart 79 takes three of the nine businesses shown on Chart 78 and illustrates each business's movement over time in terms of its profitability measured by the correlation between return on assets and return on spending. Placing each business on its own grid is less confusing than placing all three on one grid. More charts? Yes. But simpler comparisons per chart.

Chart 80. Oops, I'd better quit while I'm ahead.

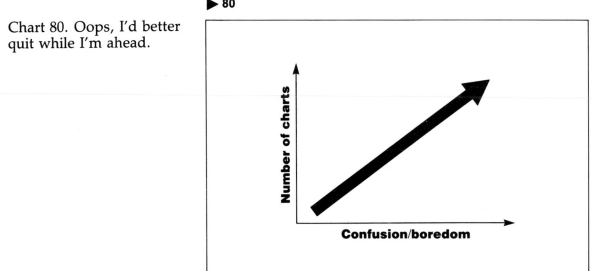

# SAYING IT WITH 35MM SLIDES

**A**s Frank was planning his charts for the presentations for the next phase of the project, he needed to decide which medium would be most appropriate for the situation. He came to my office to discuss the options. Here's the conversation.

FRANK     Gene, if I had my way, the ideal visual aid would be prepared from any size original. It would be inexpensive to produce, yet sharp and clear in color or black and white. It would lend itself to quick and easy revision and production with any available copying equipment. It would be projectable in any size room with bright lights and legible to any size audience from 1 to 1,000. And finally, it would measure 2 inches by 2 inches when you carry it but 8½ inches by 11 inches when you use it. Since nothing with all those qualities exists, what are my options?

GENE Z.   Putting aside film and video, the choice comes down to either lap visuals—also called sit-down presentations or decks—or overhead transparencies or 35mm slides. Each has its place. None should be thought of as a substitute for the others.

**Lap visuals,** either loose sheets or bound paper copies of visuals distributed to each member of the audience, are best used to generate interaction with not more than four people. Typically, the purpose is to discuss your work to date, to check the accuracy of facts, to bring up issues, to test conclusions, to build consensus for recommendations, to gain commitment to action programs. Sitting around a table makes everyone an equal partner in the discussion.

**Overhead transparencies** are best for audiences of 4 to 20, although I've used them for larger audiences. In this type of presentation, you generally stand up and take a leadership role for the presentation. However, audience participation isn't ruled out. Because you can change the sequence of visuals, omit transparencies, and keep the room lights on, you have the flexibility you want for an interactive presentation.

**35mm slides** or transparencies can be used with audiences of 20 to 50 people, depending on the amount of interaction you want. With more than 50 people, you're better off with 35mm slides. In this situation, you're probably standing at a lectern equipped with a microphone. Because you're confined by the sequence of the slides in the tray and the room is usually darkened, few if any questions are likely to be raised during the presentation. As a result, 35mm presentations are best reserved for "pure" presentations or speeches.

FRANK   What's all the noise I've been hearing about multimedia?

GENE Z.   **Multimedia** provides a degree of flexibility that is not available with any other visual aid. Think of it as a computer-based slide show with sound, and/or with video, and/or with animation. Think of it as an interactive presentation tool that lets you move along any branch of a *story tree*, instead of locking you into the linearity of a *story line*. At the same time, think of it in terms of longer and more expensive preparation time. Also, between you and me, I'm not that comfortable with the technology and the expertise it takes to project it successfully, so I bring backup transparencies to my presentations . . . just in case.

FRANK    Sounds promising. I'll look for opportunities to use it. For now, though, let's go back to our discussion of the more conventional tools. Tell me, is there a difference in impact between overhead transparencies and 35mm slides?

GENE Z.    It's a subtle, but important difference. With overhead transparencies, since the room lights are on and you have the flexibility to use a given visual or not and to change the sequence, the audience's attention is focused more on *you* as the source of the message than on the visuals that help you tell the story. Think of a television news broadcaster: you're aware of the speaker; he or she establishes eye contact with you and, on occasion, uses visuals behind his or her shoulder to support, emphasize, and demonstrate a news item.

With 35mm slides, given the darkened room, the audience's attention is on the parade of *visuals;* you, or more accurately, your voice, provide background commentary on what the audience should look for. Think of a travelogue: you focus on the scenic beauty and excitement of Paris, while some behind-the-scenes voice describes what you see.

FRANK    Am I to understand that 35mm slides make for a more formal presentation?

GENE Z.    It's more a matter of interaction than formality. It's not the *medium* that dictates formality, rather it's *you* the speaker—the tone of your voice, the language you use—who sets the degree of formality. If you choose to, you can set a formal tone with overheads and an informal tone with 35mm slides.

FRANK    That settles it. I used overhead transparencies last week with the steering committee because I needed to create interaction and be responsive to questions as they came up. Now that the committee has approved the recommendations, the chairman has asked me to present them to the regions as the basis for the company's strategic plans for the 1990s. I expect large audiences and few questions, so let's say it with 35mm slides. By the way, I've seen some very dramatic visual effects created with 35mm slides. How are these accomplished? Should I use them?

GENE Z.   You're probably referring to a system called either "speed dissolve" or "lapse dissolve," and you've probably seen it at Disneyland or at the World's Fair or at large industry conventions.

With the typical single-projector setup, the slide-change mechanism leaves the screen blank while the carousel lifts the previous slide and advances to the next slide before dropping it and projecting it. With a dissolve system, two or more projectors are hooked in tandem through a black box. With this setup, the light from one projector shuts off while the light from the companion turns on. The effect is that as one slide fades off, the other fades on. The results are indeed exciting. You can simulate animation or use succeeding slides like the overlays on transparencies.

However, this technique requires the kind of care in preparation that only experienced professionals can take. The artwork for the slides must be carefully registered so the transition from one slide to the next is imperceptible to the audience; the projectors must be aligned so the images mesh perfectly; the projection bulbs must be of the same brightness level.

For your type of presentation, I would avoid this kind of special effect: it distracts even more from you as the speaker and it risks the accusation that you're more concerned with style than with substance. Besides, if you can't get your message across with one projector, two won't help. Also, much more can go wrong with the presentation; one slide that jams, one bulb that blows is enough to deal with.

FRANK   That makes sense. I'll keep it simple. Any thoughts of how to design the slides?

GENE Z.   I thought you'd never ask.

Designing 35mm slides requires patience that borders on the heroic. We're talking about designing visuals that must ultimately fit in an area of 1.3 inches by 0.9 inches, regardless of the size of the original we start with, while retaining legibility no matter how large the audience.

Take a look at the visuals I've prepared to emphasize the constraint. Visual 1a shows what a complex chart looks like on a sheet of paper. Visual 1b shows the effect of reducing the same chart to fit on a 35mm slide. We can clearly see that the results would not be legible regardless of the size of the screen or the viewing distance.

▶ 1b

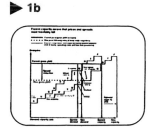

▶ 1a

## Excess capacity means that prices and spreads must inevitably fall

━━━━━━  Current price (gross yield on loans)
■ ■ ■ ■ ■  New price following entry of lower-cost competitors
━━━━━━  Current competitors' cost curve (includes interest expense, cost of equity, operating costs, and loan loss provisions)

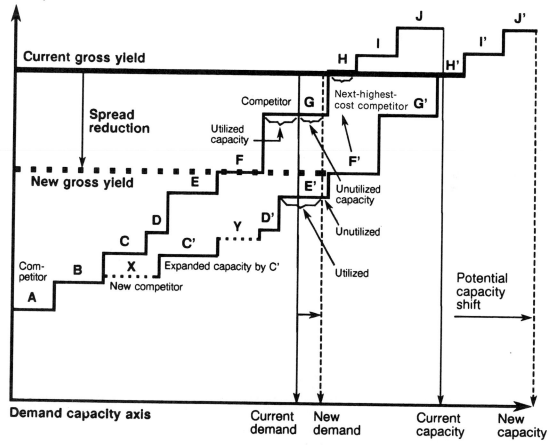

Note: C',D',etc., denotes competitors' changed position

133

In short, it's oversimplifying to say that a 35mm slide is a reduced version of a visual in a handout or an overhead transparency. We need to take a drastically different approach: less per slide, much less; and more slides, many more.

Here is how I would recommend presenting the same information using 35mm slides to a business audience that might be unfamiliar with the cost curve concept. The key to simplifying this and other complex charts is to present one idea per slide, rather than six ideas on one slide. Talk or write out the individual ideas that make up the story the exhibits tell—in the sequence in which you will relate them. Then visualize each idea on a separate slide. For example:

The point we want to make at this stage of our presentation is that
**excess capacity will inevitably lead to price declines and narrower spreads.**
Let me show you why.

Idea ▶ **1.** First, we show
the current situation. On
the vertical axis at the left,
we show the cost, and
on the horizontal axis, the
capacity. The steps of the
column chart represent the
companies in this
industry.

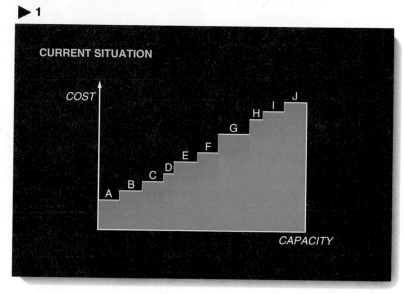

Idea ▶ **2.** Against that
profile we show the
current demand and
the current price line.
The difference be-
tween price and the
respective company
costs equals the
current spread.

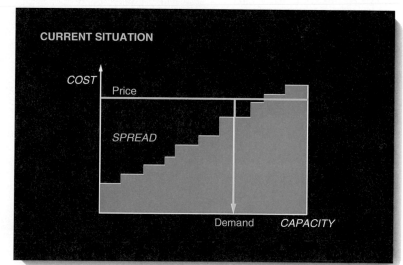

*Time passes and the profile changes.*

Idea ▶ **3.** Now we have
new, low-cost compet-
itors, and we have some
existing competitors
who have added capacity,
so the industry profile
has changed.

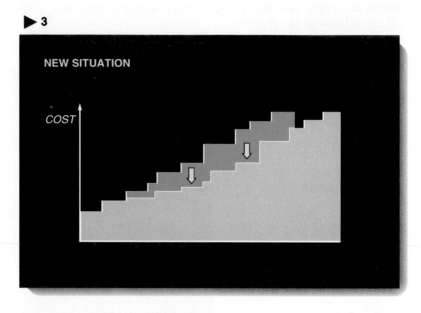

Idea ▶ **4.** The result is
an increase in unutilized
capacity.

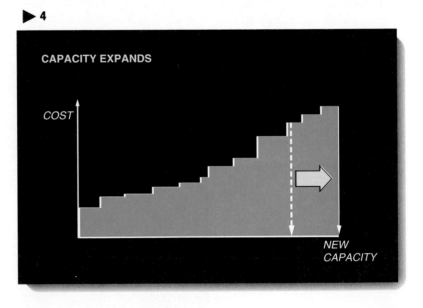

Idea ▶ **5.** As a result, prices fall and . . .

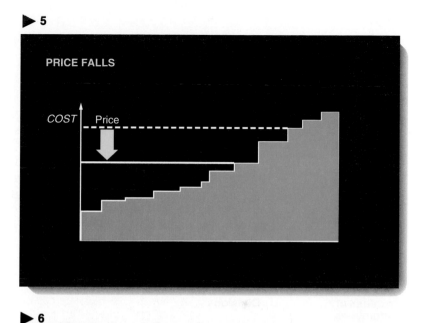

Idea ▶ **6.** Demand expands, which leads, as you would expect, to narrower spreads.

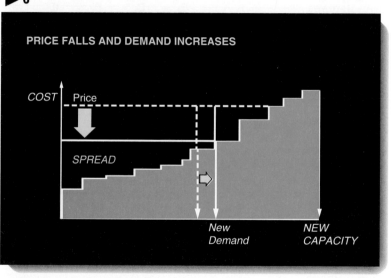

Resist the idea that more slides mean a longer presentation. It doesn't work that way because it takes as much time to discuss six ideas on one slide as it does to discuss one idea on each of six slides. What follows are similar examples you may want to refer to the next time you need to translate charts that may have worked well on paper—or transparencies—into 35mm slides.

# LESS IS BETTER

This table shows 8 headings across the page and lists 10 entries down the side, resulting in a matrix of 80 bits of information. While such a detailed table may have a place in the appendix of a report, it must be simplified to work in a visual presentation.

## A high percentage of employees hold degrees

| Number of employees with degrees | Divisions | | | | | | |
|---|---|---|---|---|---|---|---|
| | A | B | C | D | E | Others | Total |
| Associate | 14 | 20 | 15 | 18 | 6 | 19 | 92 |
| Bachelor of Arts | 7 | 12 | 1 | 6 | 9 | 23 | 58 |
| Bachelor of Science | 20 | 18 | 8 | 19 | 15 | 13 | 93 |
| Master of Arts | | 1 | | | 1 | 5 | 7 |
| Master of Science | 4 | 1 | | 5 | 2 | 5 | 17 |
| Ph.D., J.D., others | | | | | | 8 | 8 |
| Total degrees* | 45 | 52 | 24 | 43 | 30 | 55 | 241 |
| Total employees | 53 | 77 | 46 | 107 | 88 | n.a. | 371 |
| Percent of employees with degrees | 85% | 68% | 52% | 40% | 34% | – | 65%** |

\* Excludes master's and advanced degrees to avoid double-counting
\** For the 5 major Divisions - excludes "All Other"
   Source:  Personnel card file; special survey of employees

▶ 1

% OF EMPLOYEES WITH DEGREES

| Total employees | | % WITH DEGREES |
|---|---|---|
| 53 | Division A | 85% |
| 77 | Division B | 68% |
| 46 | Division C | 52% |
| 107 | Division D | 40% |
| 88 | Division E | 34% |
| | | TOTAL 65% |

For 35mm slides, the answer is to visualize the message the title states: "a high percentage of employees hold degrees." If it is important to discuss the kinds of degrees the employees hold, design a second slide of the types of degrees and leave the data in tabular form.

▶ 2

NUMBER OF EMPLOYEES WITH DEGREES

| DEGREES | DIVISIONS | | | | | |
|---|---|---|---|---|---|---|
| | A | B | C | D | E | Others |
| Associate | 14 | 20 | 15 | 18 | 6 | 19 |
| B.A. | 7 | 12 | 1 | 6 | 9 | 23 |
| B.S. | 20 | 18 | 8 | 19 | 15 | 13 |
| M.A. | | 1 | | | 1 | 5 |
| M.S. | 4 | 1 | | 5 | 2 | 5 |
| Advanced | | | | | | 8 |

## SIMPLER IS BETTER

This chart was used as an overhead transparency in a visual presentation to support the point that PVC is the lowest-cost polymer and is lower in cost than all but two metals.

*For 35mm slides, the content must be simplified. For example:*

¶ Do we need two measures of cost performance to support the same message—one expressed in cents per pound, the other in cents per cubic inch? No. Cents per pound will do.

¶ Do we need the ranges of cost shown for some of the items? No. Would averages be OK? Yes.

## Current cost of PVC is competitive with other materials

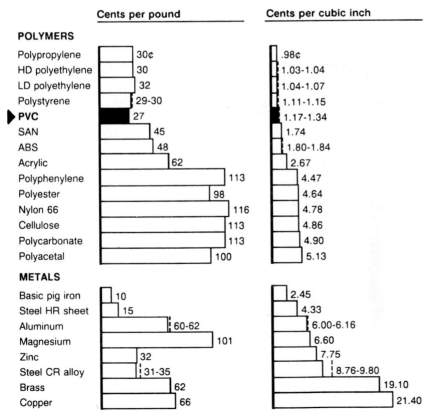

¶ Must we show the data at the end of every bar?
No. A scale will be sufficient to see the relationships.

¶ Because this is an item comparison, can we change
the sequence of the bars, ranking them from high to
low to better show PVC's position? Yes.

Combining the answers results in two simple slides:

Slide ▶ **1.**
Shows PVC's cost
position against all
other polymers.

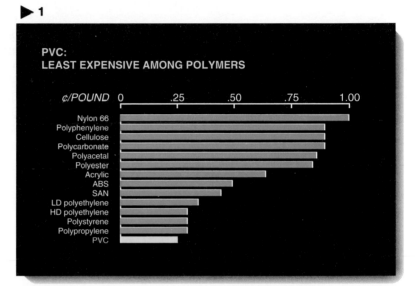

Slide ▶ **2.**
Shows PVC's cost
position against
metals.

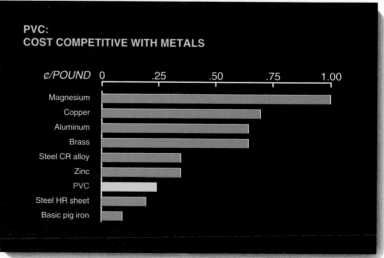

## DIFFERENT IS BETTER

At times, splitting a detailed chart into several slides isn't the answer; simplifying the story can result in a single slide.

This series of item comparisons shows that the Tuckahoe plant is doing an excellent job of keeping variable costs low in the manufacture of three out of four products. For HFCS-42 and HFCS-55, it ranks as the second-lowest-cost producer. While it ranks fourth for pearl starch, the cost differential with the lowest-cost plant is small. However, for corn syrup, the combination of a seventh ranking and a sizable cost differential indicates the need to search for cost-reduction opportunities.

# VARIABLE MANUFACTURING COST PER PLANT
Dollars per hundred weight

## HFCS - 42

| | Corn | Processing | Total |
|---|---|---|---|
| Clinton | $4.79 | $1.27 | $6.06 |
| ▶ Tuckahoe | 4.85 | 1.31 | 6.16 |
| Decatur | 4.94 | 1.31 | 6.25 |
| Lafayette | 5.10 | 1.30 | 6.40 |
| Geneva | 4.89 | 1.58 | 6.47 |
| Argo | 4.85 | 1.69 | 6.54 |
| Cedar Rapids | 4.89 | 1.68 | 6.57 |
| Lafayette | 5.38 | 1.32 | 6.70 |
| Johnstown | 5.08 | 1.66 | 6.74 |
| Dayton | 5.12 | 1.73 | 6.85 |
| Montezuma | 5.02 | 1.84 | 6.86 |
| Loudon | 5.44 | 1.43 | 6.87 |
| Memphis | 5.40 | 1.60 | 7.00 |
| Plainstown | 5.67 | 1.39 | 7.06 |
| Morrisville | 5.48 | 1.78 | 7.26 |
| Salem | 5.73 | 1.62 | 7.35 |
| Dimmit | 5.78 | 1.58 | 7.36 |
| Stockton | 5.48 | 2.21 | 7.69 |
| Tracy | 5.60 | 2.32 | 7.92 |

## HFCS - 55

| | Corn | Processing | Total |
|---|---|---|---|
| Clinton | $5.02 | $1.45 | $6.47 |
| ▶ Tuckahoe | 5.08 | 1.76 | 6.84 |
| Decatur | 5.13 | 1.92 | 7.05 |
| Lafayette | 5.35 | 1.78 | 7.13 |
| Cedar Rapids | 5.13 | 2.08 | 7.21 |
| Johnston | 5.32 | 1.96 | 7.28 |
| Dayton | 5.37 | 2.16 | 7.53 |
| Memphis | 5.65 | 1.97 | 7.62 |
| Loudon | 5.70 | 1.98 | 7.68 |
| Plainstown | 5.94 | 1.91 | 7.85 |
| Salem | 6.01 | 1.97 | 7.98 |
| Dimmit | 6.05 | 2.01 | 8.06 |
| Morrisville | 5.74 | 2.51 | 8.25 |

## PEARL STARCH

| | Corn | Processing | Total |
|---|---|---|---|
| Cedar Rapids | $6.53 | $.59 | $7.11 |
| Muscatine | 6.61 | .58 | 7.20 |
| Argo | 6.58 | .66 | 7.24 |
| ▶ Tuckahoe | 6.58 | .68 | 7.26 |
| Cedar Rapids | 6.64 | .68 | 7.32 |
| Decatur | 6.70 | .64 | 7.34 |
| Cedar Rapids | 6.64 | .88 | 7.52 |
| Hammond | 6.95 | .63 | 7.58 |
| Dayton | 6.95 | .80 | 7.75 |
| Lafayette | 7.30 | .69 | 7.99 |
| Geneva | 7.70 | .84 | 8.54 |
| Dimmit | 7.84 | .86 | 8.70 |
| Salem | 7.78 | .93 | 8.71 |
| Morrisville | 7.44 | 1.34 | 8.78 |
| Stockton | 7.44 | 1.50 | 8.94 |

## CORN SYRUP

| | Corn | Processing | Total |
|---|---|---|---|
| Johnstown | $5.73 | $.54 | $6.30 |
| Cedar Rapids | 5.83 | .54 | 6.37 |
| Decatur | 5.83 | .60 | 6.43 |
| Geneva | 5.88 | .57 | 6.45 |
| Plainstown | 5.83 | .66 | 6.49 |
| Argo | 5.78 | .83 | 6.61 |
| ▶ Tuckahoe | 5.78 | .83 | 6.61 |
| Lafayette | 6.08 | .54 | 6.62 |
| Dayton | 6.10 | .66 | 6.76 |
| Hammond | 6.10 | .76 | 6.86 |
| Lafayette | 6.40 | .59 | 6.99 |
| Memphis | 6.43 | .59 | 7.02 |
| Kansas City | 6.28 | .83 | 7.11 |

Slides ▶ **1** to **4.** For 35mm slides, the most obvious solution would seem to be to use a separate slide for each product, simplify each slide by showing only the totals, and substitute a scale for the figures at the end of the bars. However, with 19 plants listed, the plant names and cost figures would be illegible.

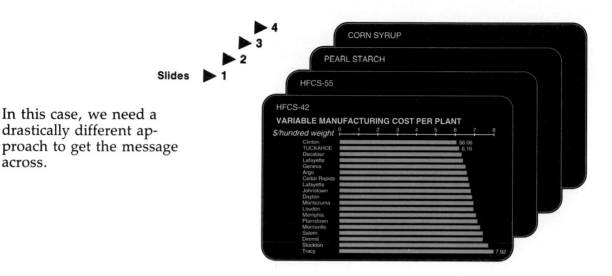

In this case, we need a drastically different approach to get the message across.

Slide ▶ 5. Let's use a range column to show the spread in total variable cost between the best and the worst performers for the four products. (I should have used a bar chart to be consistent with my advice in the earlier chapter. Somehow the column chart is more suggestive of "best" at the top and "worst" at the bottom.) In this example, the ranges are of the same length, creating an index chart; that is, the spread equals 100 regardless of cost differentials. I show Tuckahoe's ranking against the top and bottom performers. The message comes across with only *one* slide.

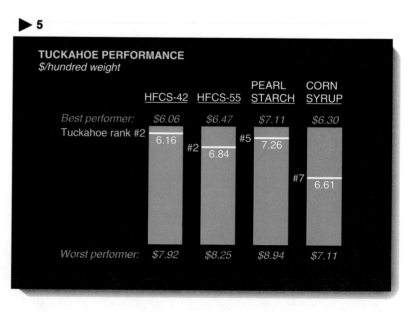

# MORE IS BETTER

This one chart provides a thoughtful study of how the sources of additions and subtractions net out to totals over time. Carried to an extreme, this type of chart reinforces Zelazny's first law of charting: "Nothing is ever so simple that it cannot be made complex." In this case, the story can be told more quickly with two simple 35mm slides.

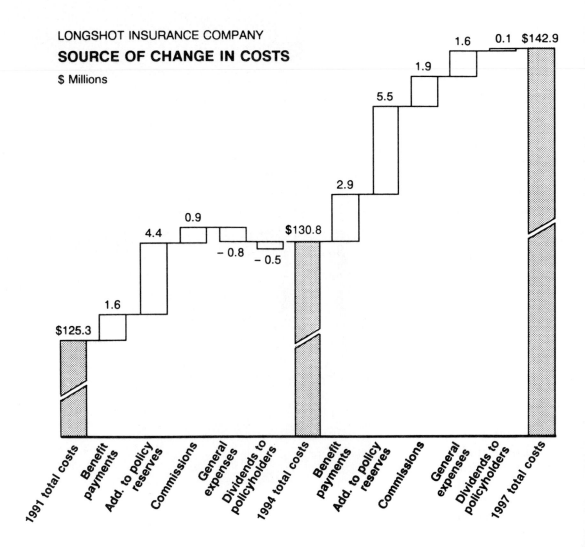

LONGSHOT INSURANCE COMPANY

**SOURCE OF CHANGE IN COSTS**

$ Millions

Slide ▶ **1.** Stress the total change in costs from 1991 to 1994 and from 1994 to 1997.

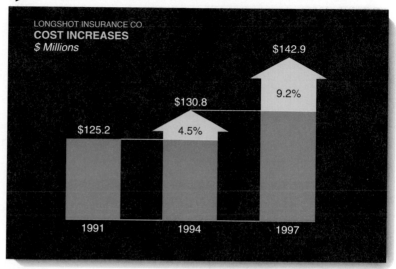

▶ 1

LONGSHOT INSURANCE CO.
**COST INCREASES**
*$ Millions*

$125.2   $130.8   $142.9

4.5%   9.2%

1991   1994   1997

Slide ▶ **2.** Compare the sources of change for the two time periods by using a simple table.

▶ 2

LONGSHOT INSURANCE CO.
**SOURCES OF CHANGE**
*$ Millions*

|  | 1991-94 | 1994-97 |
|---|---|---|
| Benefit payments | $1.6 | $2.9 |
| Addition to policy reserves | 4.4 | 5.5 |
| Commissions | 0.9 | 1.9 |
| General expenses | −0.8 | 1.6 |
| Dividends | −0.5 | 0.1 |
| *NET CHANGE* | *$5.6* | *$12.0* |

## BOLD IS BETTER

The temptation to make one 35mm slide of this visual should be resisted; it won't be legible. The first thing that comes to mind is to make six slides: one for each comparison between J.J. Ltd. and one of its competitors. However, in this case, the message is: **"Five out of six competitors have outperformed J.J. Ltd. since 1993."**

## Five out of six competitors have outperformed J.J. Ltd. since 1993

## Total operating income

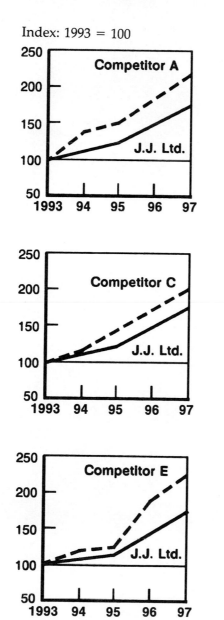
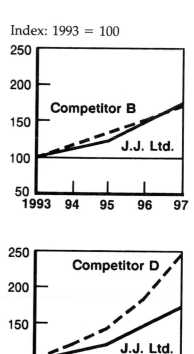
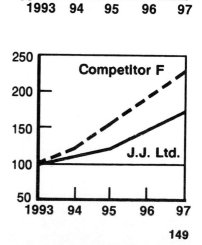

*The options are:*

**A.** Show all trends on one slide, while emphasizing **J.J. Ltd.** with a bolder or different-colored trend line.

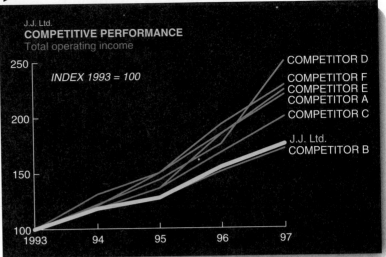

**B.** Assuming that the intervening hiccups in the various trends are unimportant, use straight lines and emphasize **J.J. Ltd.**

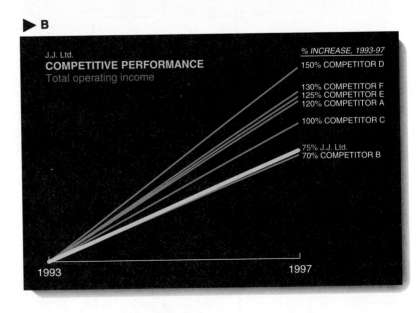

**C.** Show the percentage increases with a bar chart; use a contrasting color for **J.J. Ltd.**

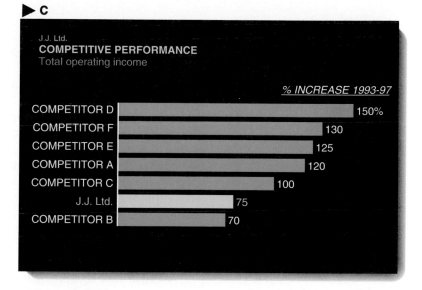

▶ **C**

J.J. Ltd.
**COMPETITIVE PERFORMANCE**
Total operating income

*% INCREASE 1993-97*

| | |
|---|---|
| COMPETITOR D | 150% |
| COMPETITOR F | 130 |
| COMPETITOR E | 125 |
| COMPETITOR A | 120 |
| COMPETITOR C | 100 |
| J.J. Ltd. | 75 |
| COMPETITOR B | 70 |

**D.** If legibility remains a problem, use a simple table; use a color for **J.J. Ltd.** that will make it stand out from the crowd.

▶ **D**

J.J. Ltd.
**COMPETITIVE PERFORMANCE**
Total operating income

| | % increase 1993-97 |
|---|---|
| COMPETITOR D | 150% |
| COMPETITOR F | 130 |
| COMPETITOR E | 125 |
| COMPETITOR A | 120 |
| COMPETITOR C | 100 |
| J.J. Ltd. | 75 |
| COMPETITOR B | 70 |

# LESSONS LEARNED

As you've seen from the examples, there is no single formula for success. In some cases, the answer is to divide the message into multiple slides; in others, to use fewer. In some cases, the answer is to change the way you tell the story; in others, to substitute tabular data for charts. In all cases, however, the trick is to be disciplined (ruthless is a better word) about removing details from the slides and to choose and use color with purpose. Let me elaborate.

## REMOVING DETAILS

¶ Round out figures; cut decimal places unless they are important to your message—you can always use the precise number in your talk.

¶ Use scales instead of numbers at the end of bars or within components of columns.

¶ Substitute symbols for words—a $ sign is better than "dollars": a % sign is better than "percentage of . . . ."

¶ Abbreviate where possible without causing confusion.

¶ Edit words: cut 10 words down to 4, 4 words to 3, 3 words to 2.

¶ Delete footnotes; introduce the information as part of what you say if it is important to mention.

¶ Omit sources; leave them for the handout.

And when all else fails, don't use a slide. Chances are that if it can't be simplified, it doesn't belong on the screen. Let's face it, Winston Churchill gave some great speeches without visual aids, and what he had to say was more important than anything we present in our business presentation.

# CHOOSING AND USING COLORS

Up to this chapter, the charts in this book achieve the desired visual impact in black and white. A good test of the effectiveness of your visuals is to see if their messages come across clearly in black and white; if they don't, color isn't going to help much. However, we do live in a world of colors, and computers have made it easy to use them for slides, so here's how to make the most of them.

### CHOOSING COLORS

I'm told that some computer graphics systems can create 8,000,000 permutations of colors, give or take a few thousand. That's 7,999,997 more than I recommend showing on a typical slide. Not only does this simplify the decision-making process for selecting colors, but it also prevents business-minded executives from thinking about how their money is being spent to make slides "jazzy" when your message is to cut cost. Besides, it usually looks better.

Generally, the professionals I work with use a black or negative background so the colors for the visual stand out. Against the black, they use cool colors such as blue and green. For emphasis, they rely on white and yellow.

Unless you're making slides of color pictures or specific colors are needed to represent a logo or a flag, leave the choice of colors to experienced specialists whom you trust. Work out guidelines with them to ensure legibility while retaining a professional image.

## USING COLORS

If the *choice* of color can be left to specialists, the *use* of color is the presenter's responsibility. Make certain to discuss each visual with the specialist so colors are used not just for decorations, but for a purpose. For instance:

¶ **To emphasize,** for example, one component of a pie chart, one segment of a bar or column, a trend line, a row of figures, words such as a title.

¶ **To identify a recurring theme,** for example, showing your company-related data in the same color throughout the presentation.

¶ **To distinguish,** for example, actual from projected, one set of bars or columns from another, one trend line from another.

¶ **To symbolize,** for example, red for losses, red for stop, yellow for proceed with caution, and green for go.

Follow the standards set in this section for the business communications you make and remember: *if a 35mm slide were the same as a transparency, there'd be no need to call it a 35mm slide. So let it be a 35mm slide.*

# SAYING IT WITH CONCEPT VISUALS

## SOLUTIONS IN SEARCH OF PROBLEMS

So far I've presented ideas for translating quantitative information into chart form. However, some nonquantitative messages present visual challenges. Among them are concepts such as *interaction*, *leverage*, *obstacles*, and *interrelationships*. Lacking, too, have been images that convey *structure*, *sequence*, and *process*.

Sensing this gap, I created, along with several talented designers, the following portfolio of visual images for use in your reports, presentations, and articles. Here are a few suggestions for making the most of them.

In searching for the visual that meets your need, use this section as a portfolio of thought starters. In a sense, the visuals are *solutions in search of a problem.* In isolation, none is right or wrong, good or bad. The appropriateness of any visual depends on its fit with the problem at hand—and that's for you to determine.

As you search for a visual solution to a communication problem, you can look at the concepts from left to right, or turn the pages around to see what the images reveal from different perspectives. You can simplify them, expand them, or otherwise play with and modify them—in short, mold them to meet your needs. Of course, once you've selected a diagram, add the words around it or inside it that bring your message home. Take a look at these examples.

## STRUCTURE VISUAL

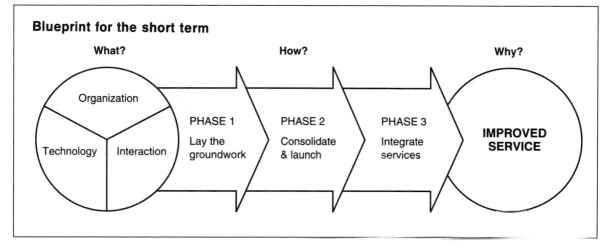

# FORCES AT WORK

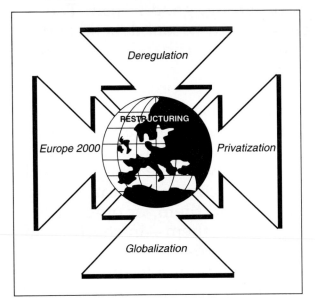

# INTERRELATIONSHIP

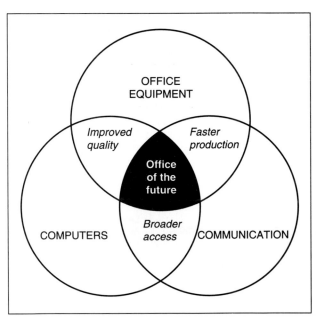

Don't necessarily settle for the first idea that grabs you. Keep looking, playing with the diagrams, creating new diagrams—so that you find the right fit. For example, let's assume that you need to visualize the following:

PROJECT PHASES
1. Plan the project
2. Startup
3. Develop solution
4. Present recommendations
5. Do it!

Here, selected from the pages of this chapter, are nine diagrams from which you might choose to visualize the process, depending on which tells your story best.

By the way, like any other visual images, these diagrams will have different meanings for different people. Therefore, I suggest you test the visual with colleagues to be sure that it clearly and easily reveals the concept you intend to convey, making sure that they understand what you want it to show.

**1**

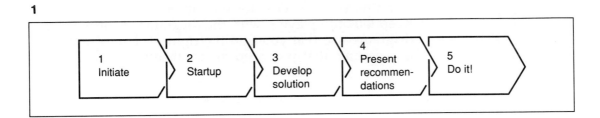

**2**

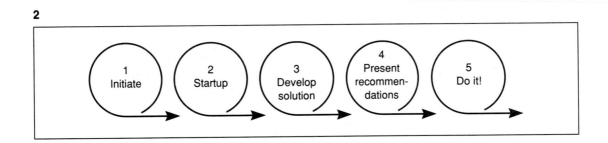

**3**

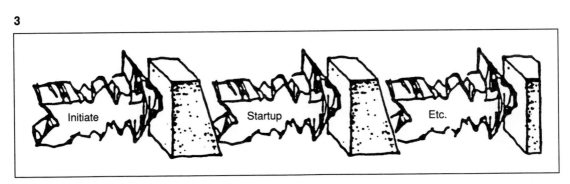

**4**

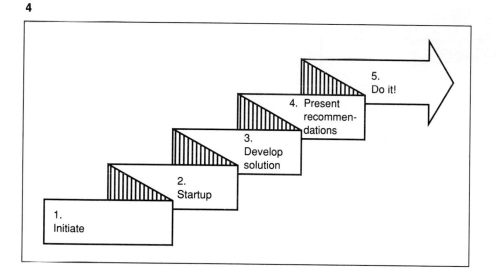

**5**

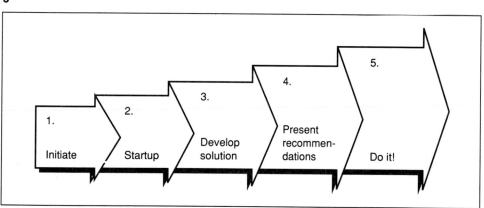

**6**

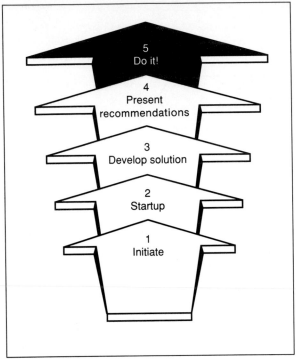

**7**

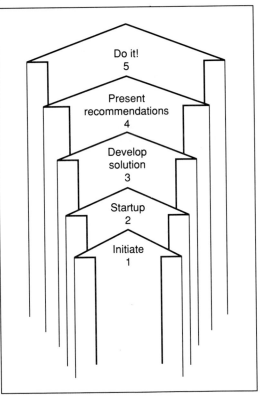

**8**

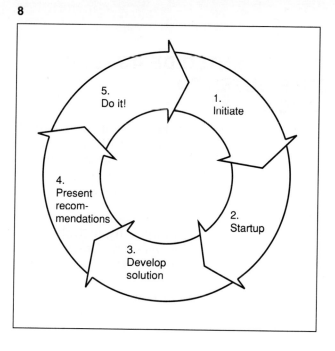

**9**

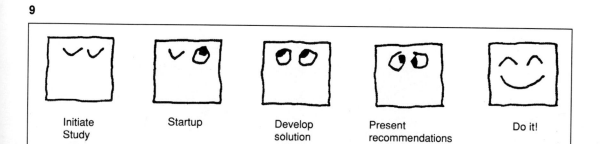

| Initiate Study | Startup | Develop solution | Present recommendations | Do it! |

## ABOUT THE TALENTED DESIGNERS
## WHO CONTRIBUTED TO
## THIS SECTION

**Jan White** is a communication design consultant who lectures worldwide on the relationship of graphics to editing. Architect by training, he was art director with Time Inc. for 13 years, then in 1964 opened his own publication design studio.

He is the author of a dozen books on visual techniques in publishing including *Editing By Design* and *Graphic Idea Notebook, Graphic Design for the Electronic Age, Color for the Electronic Age,* and recently, *Color for Impact.*

**Vera Deutsch** is known as well for her graphic design for publications as for her corporate identity programs, which range from the design of mailing labels to the creation of annual reports. Notice that she is the graphic consultant for the design of this book.

**Dan Nevins** is a freelance cartoonist. He was formerly a staff artist for the American Management Association and later Art Director of the advertising department at the New York Daily News.

**Peter Weishar** has been a professional designer and art director for over 10 years, working in publishing and advertising. Currently, he is the Creative Director of a multimedia firm specializing in commercial CD-ROM titles. Also, he is an instructor in the New York University Interactive Telecommunications Program.

# LINEAR FLOWS

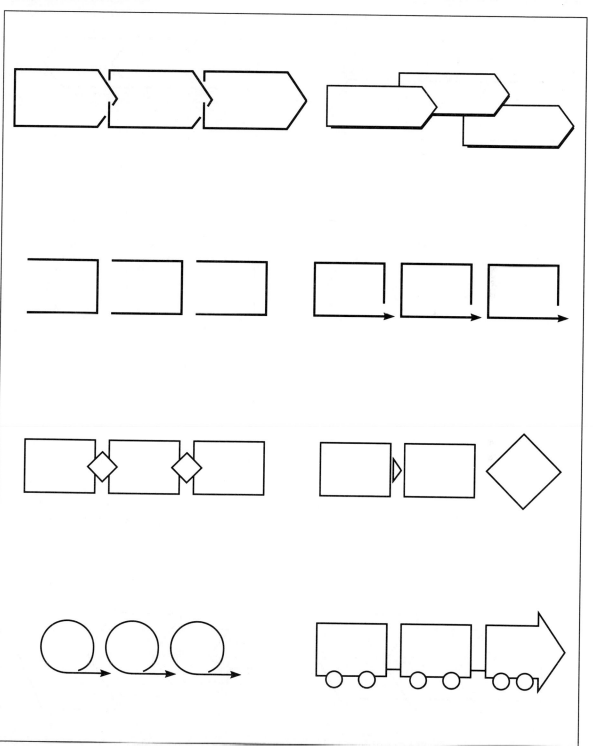

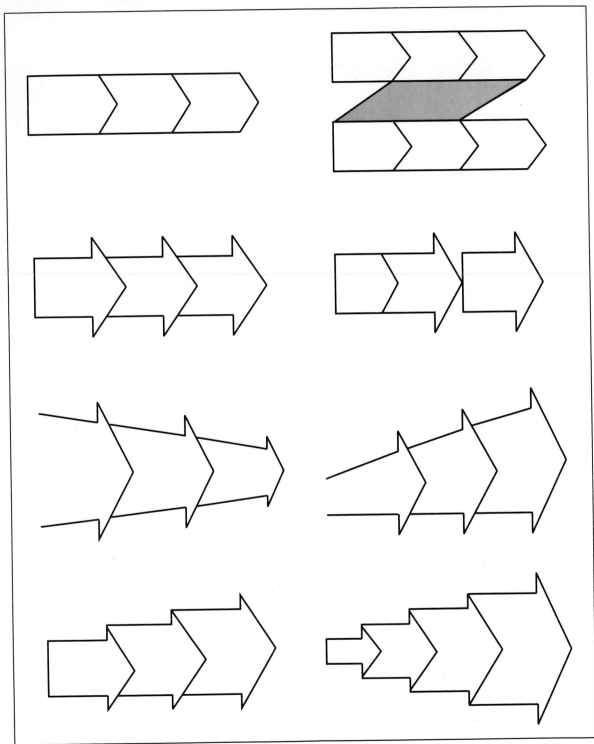

# LINEAR FLOWS

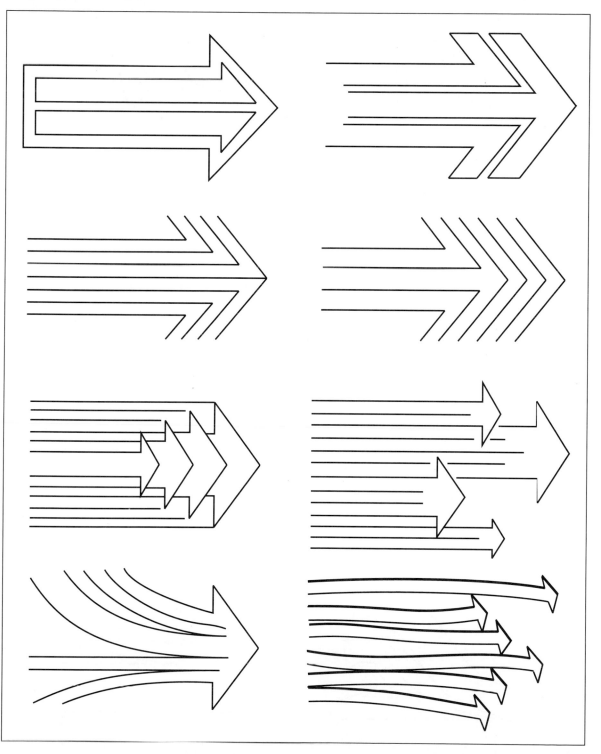

# VERTICAL FLOWS

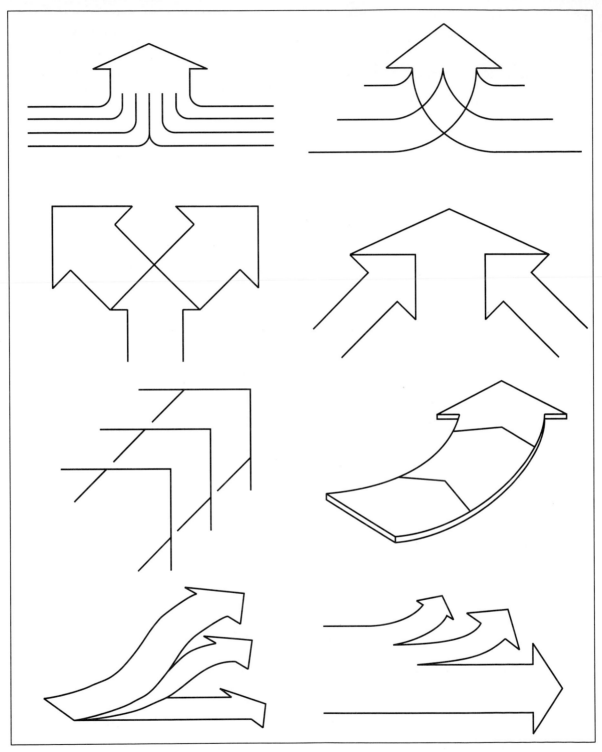

# VERTICAL FLOWS

# CIRCULAR FLOWS

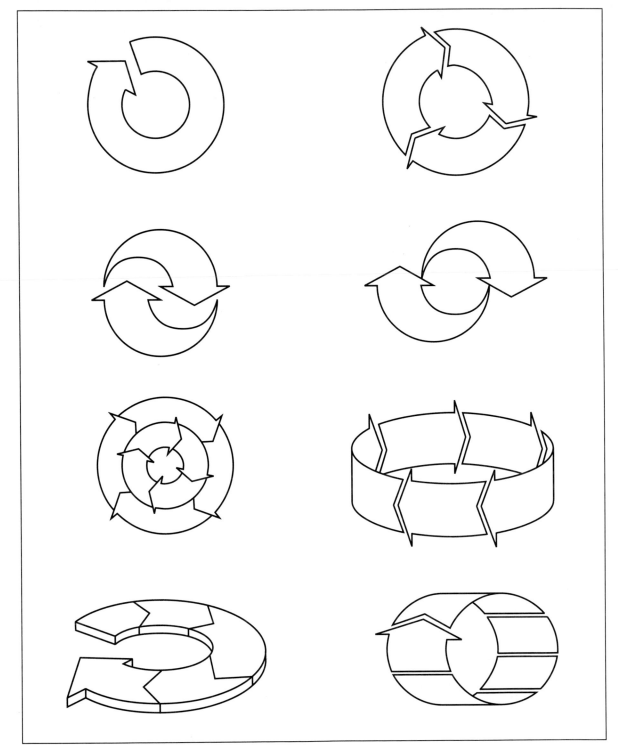

# CIRCULAR FLOWS

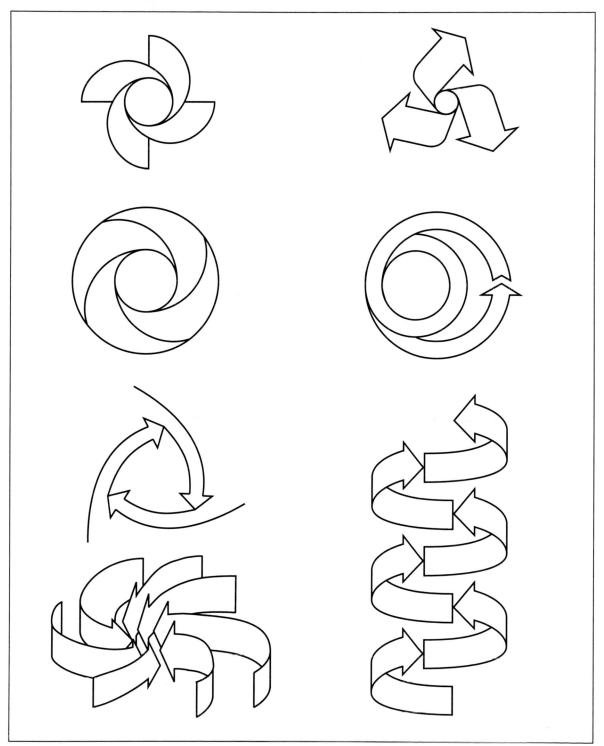

# CIRCULAR FLOWS

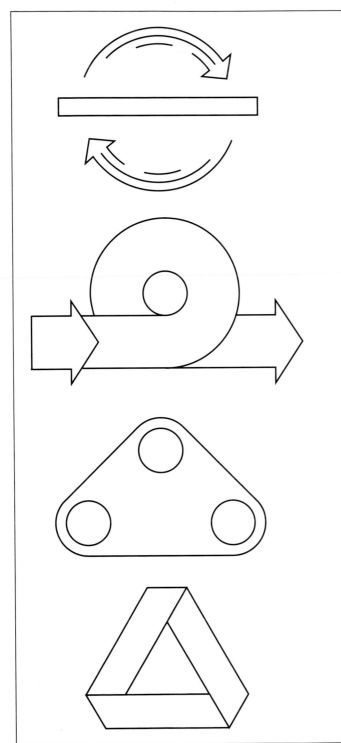

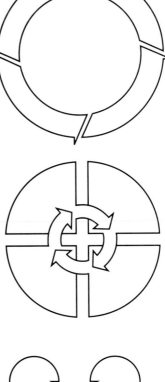

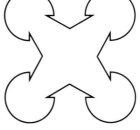

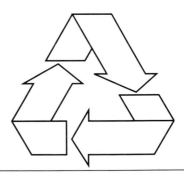

# CIRCULAR FLOWS

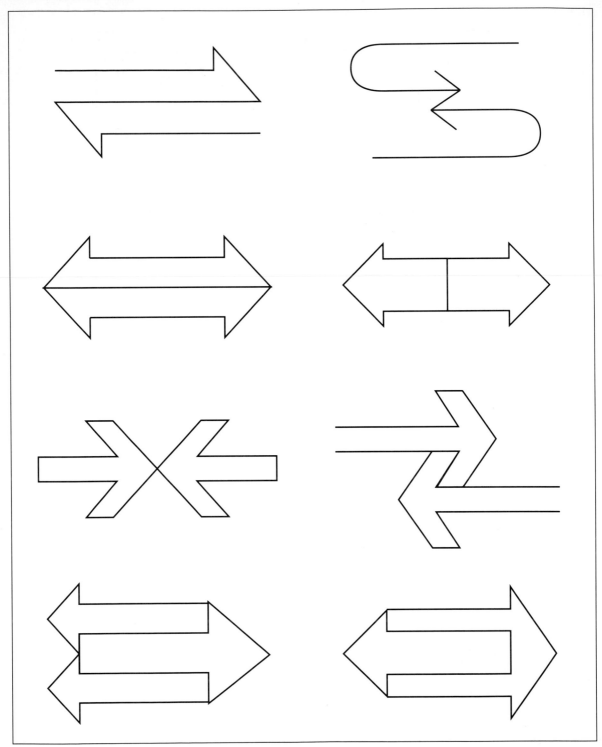

# INTERACTION

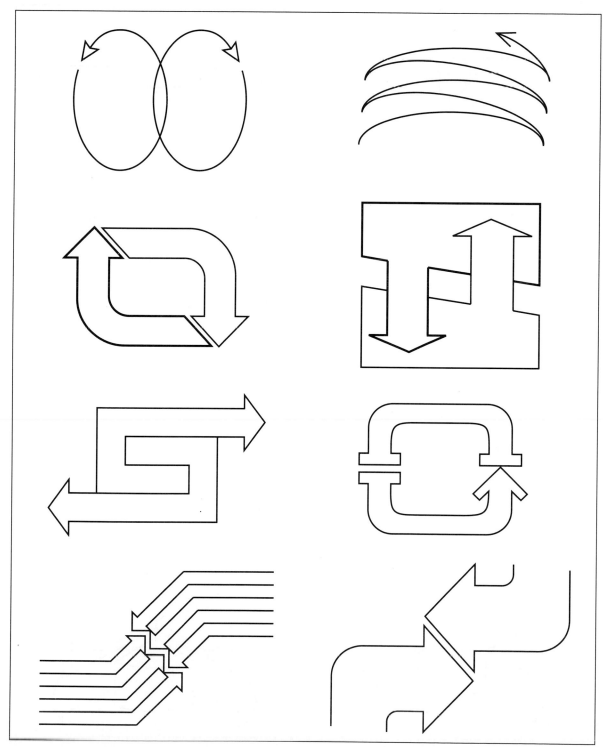

# INTERACTION

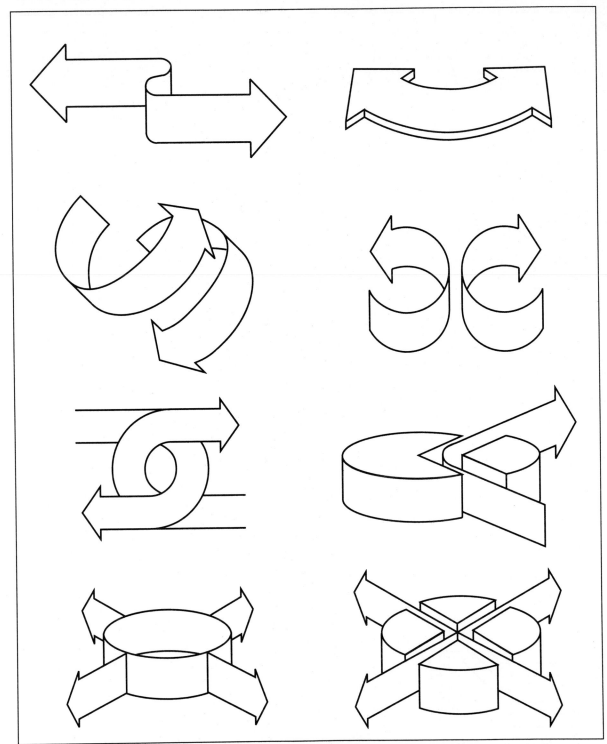

# FORCES AT WORK

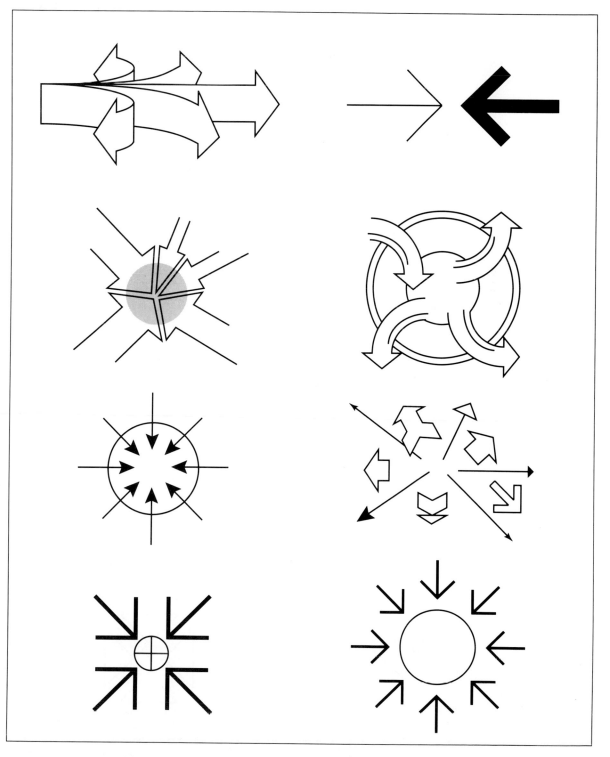

# FORCES AT WORK

# FORCES AT WORK

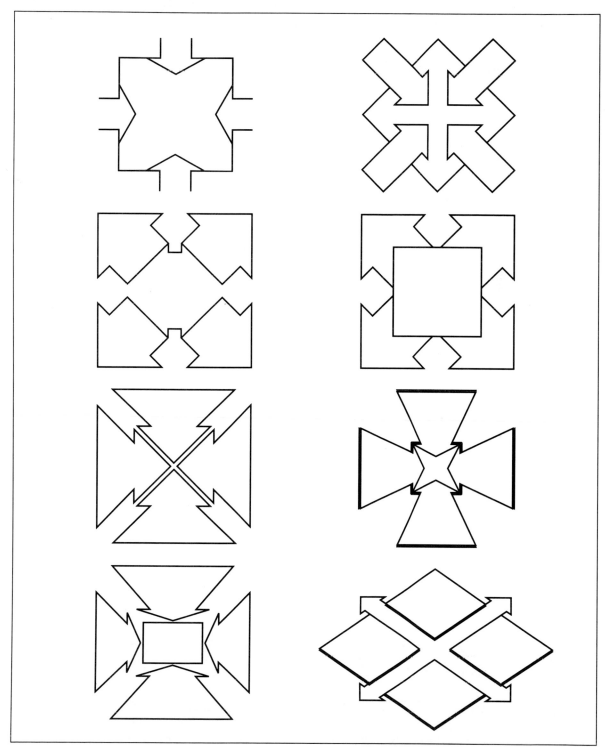

# FORCES AT WORK

# CHANGING COURSE

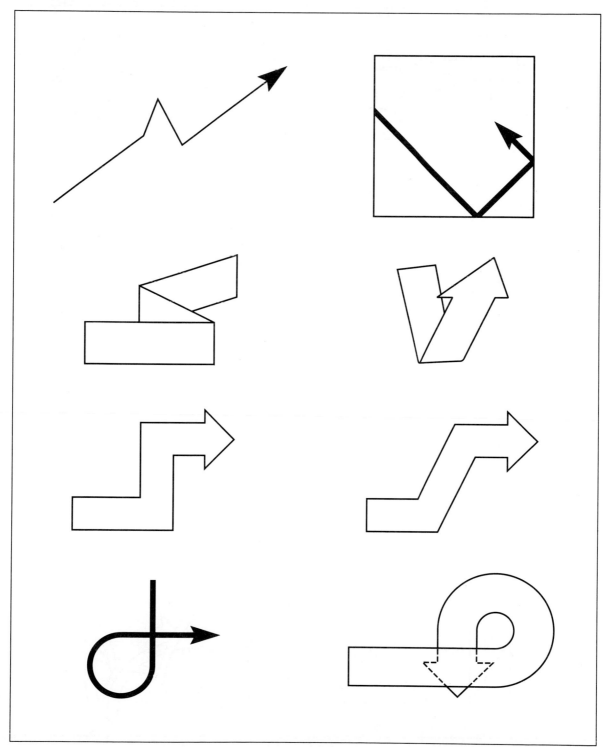

# CHANGING COURSE

# LEVERAGE/BALANCE

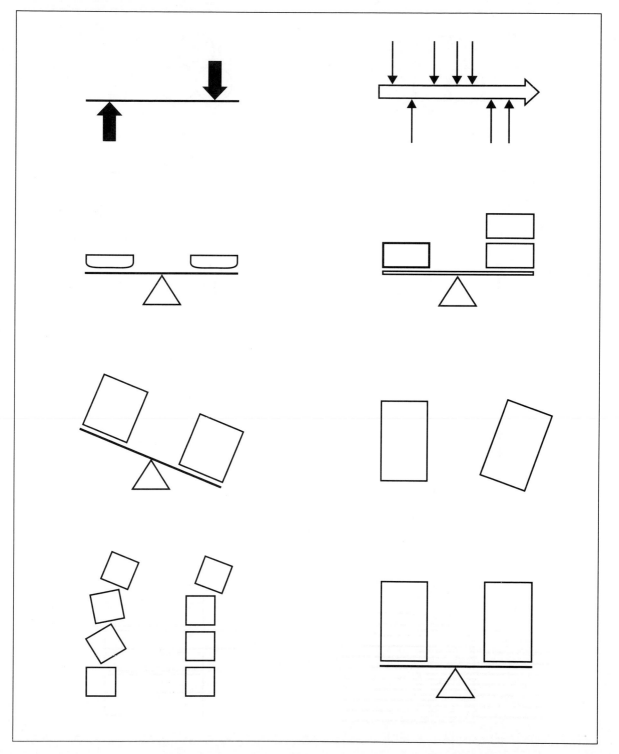

# LEVERAGE/BALANCE

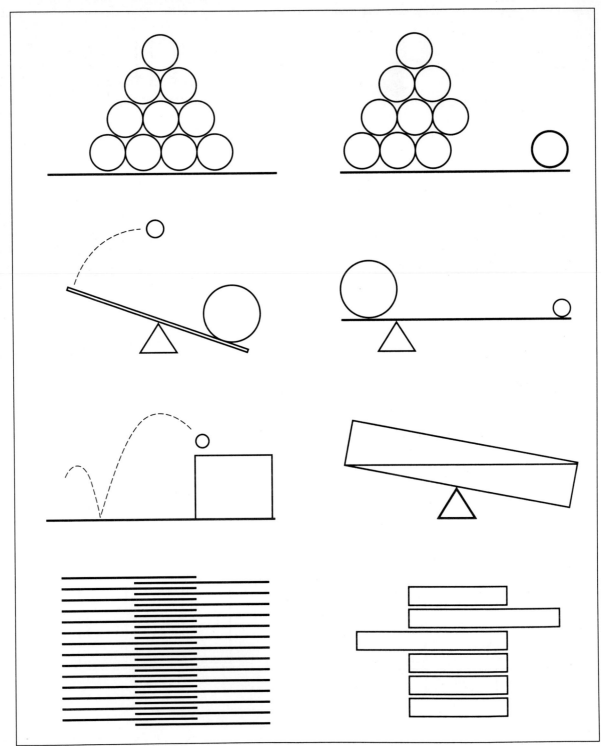

# PENETRATION/BARRIERS

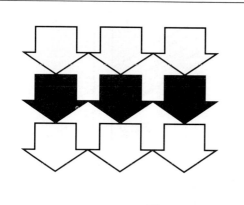

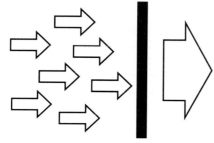

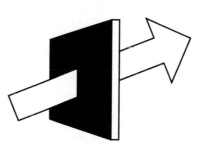

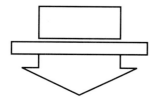

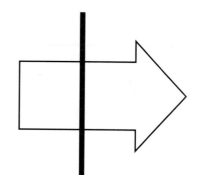

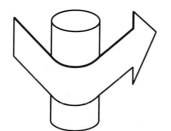

# FILTERS/SCREENS

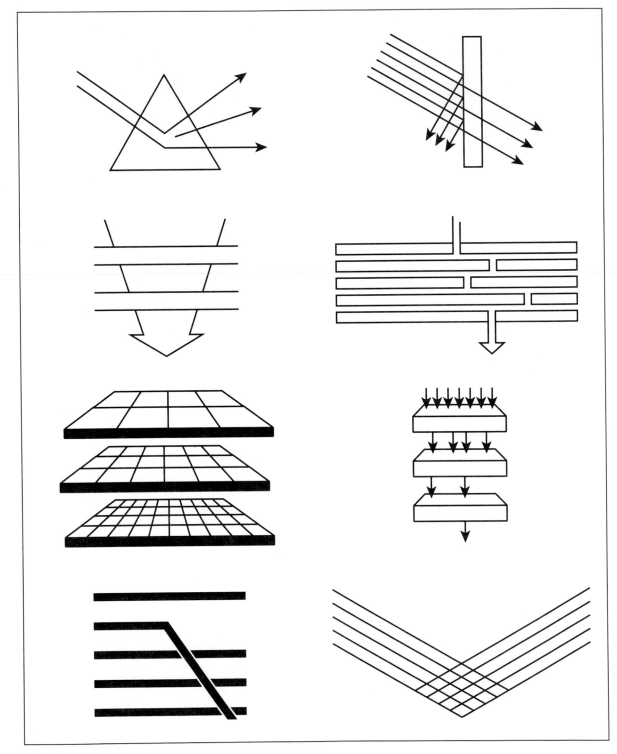

# INTERRELATIONSHIPS

## INTERRELATIONSHIPS

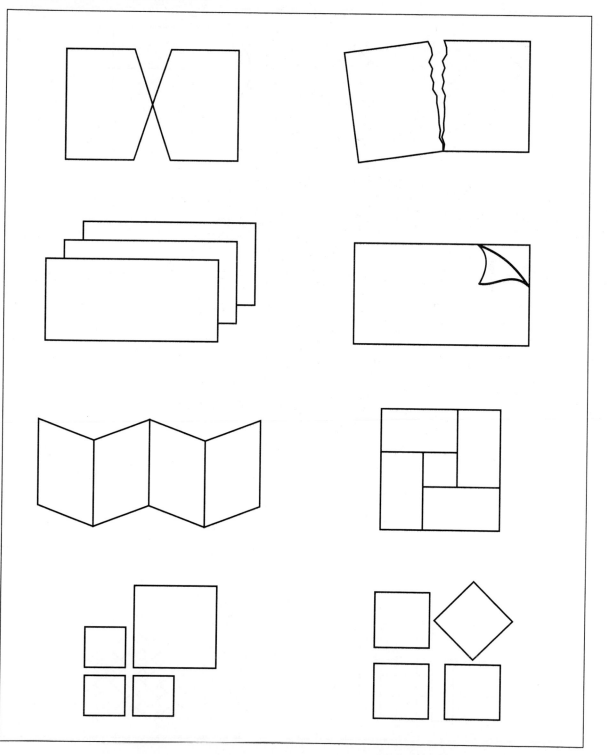

# INTERRELATIONSHIPS

# PROCESSES

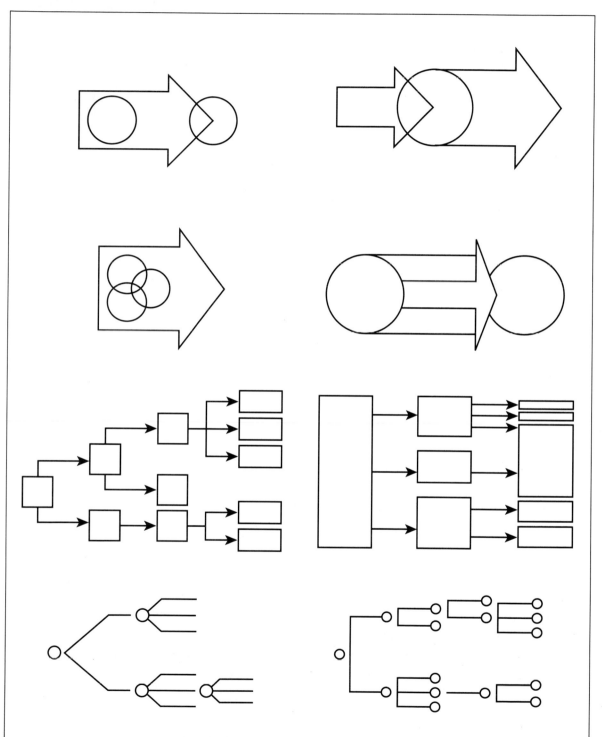

# SEGMENTATIONS

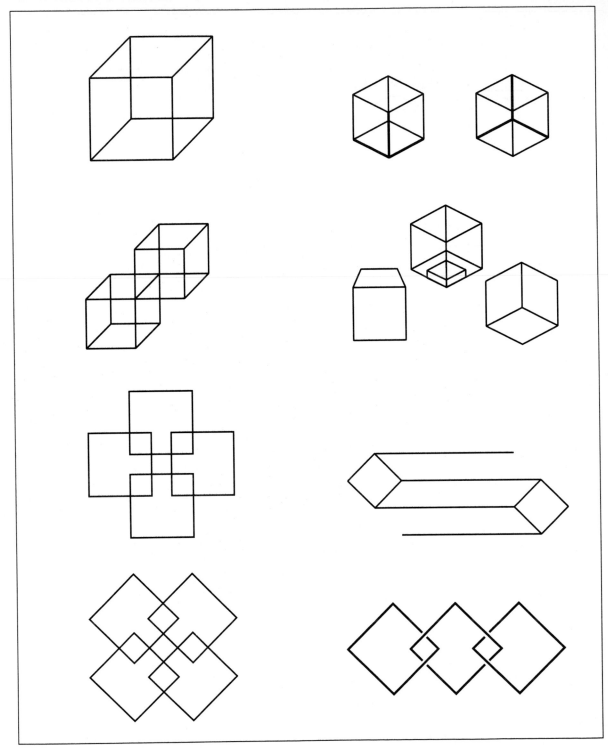

# SEGMENTATIONS

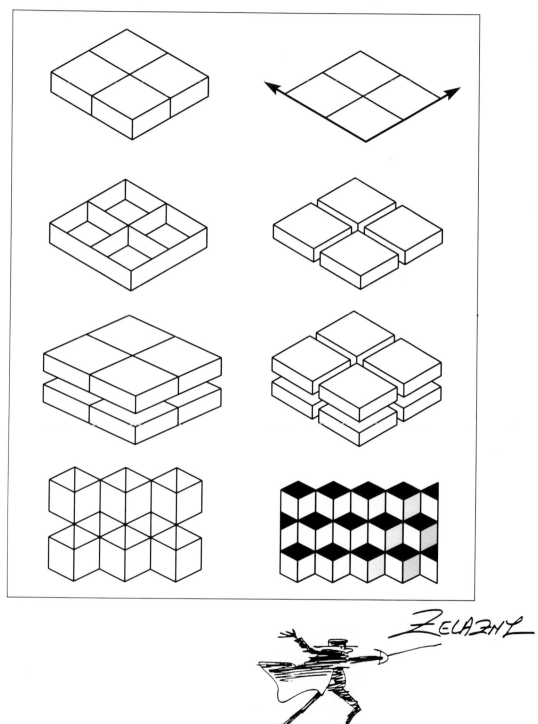

# INDEX

# ABOUT GENE ZELAZNY

**Gene Zelazny** is the Director of Visual Communications for McKinsey & Company.

Since joining the Firm in 1961, Gene has provided creative advice and assistance to the professional staff in the design of visual presentations and written reports, which has included planning the communication strategy; structuring the story line; interpreting data or concepts and recommending the best visual formats in terms of charts, diagrams, etc.; designing storyboards; and rehearsing the presenters. Also, he has designed and led communication training programs throughout the Firm.

On behalf of the Firm, Gene regularly presents his ideas for *Making The Most of Your Business Presentation* at business schools including Berkeley, Carnegie Mellon, Columbia, Cornell, Darden, Harvard, Michigan, MIT, North Carolina, Stanford, Tuck, UCLA, and Wharton in the United States, and INSEAD, London Business School, and Oxford in Europe.

Otherwise, you'll find him on a tennis court or on a bicycle, designing chess sets and sponsoring children to do the same, writing essays for his friends, and always holding hands with Judy.